THE PEBBLES ON THE BEACH

THE PEBBLES
ON THE BEACH

by

Clarence Ellis

FABER AND FABER LIMITED
3 Queen Square
London

First published in 1954
by Faber and Faber Limited
3 Queen Square, London, W.C.1.
First published in this edition 1965
Reprinted 1966, 1967, 1968, 1969, 1971 and 1972
Printed in Great Britain by
Latimer Trend & Co Ltd Whitstable
All rights reserved

ISBN 0 571 06814 6 (Faber Paper Covered Editions)

ISBN 0 571 06543 0 (Hand Bound Edition)

CONTENTS

ILLUSTRATIONS

COLOUR PLATES
between pages 64 *and* 65

1–8. A group of eight common stones representing the three classes of rock: igneous, sedimentary and metamorphic. Two polished faces, granite and schist, are shown

9–16. Another representative group of eight stones, some of which (serpentine, jet, dolerite and basalt) are less familiar. Note the contrast between the polished and unpolished surfaces of the red serpentine and the dolerite

17–27. A group of eleven semi-precious stones of which eight have been cut and polished

28–36. Of these nine stones all but the green serpentine and the gabbro are members of the quartz family or show quartz veining

INTRODUCTION

Most people collect something or other: stamps, butter-flies, beetles, moths, dried and pressed wild flowers, old snuff-boxes, china dogs and so forth. A few eccentrics even collect disused bus tickets! But collectors of pebbles are rare.

Let us hasten to add that we mean discriminating collectors. Before the authorities responsible for the preservation of our coasts awoke to the seriousness of coastal erosion, collection in its worst and widest sense went on. Hundreds of thousands of tons of shingle were removed from the beaches annually in cartloads for building and other purposes, thus depriving the cliffs of their defence against the attacks of the waves. The disastrous flooding of the East Coast in January 1953 has ensured still keener vigilance in the maintenance of natural defensive barriers.

The discriminating pebble-collector does not strive to become a pack-animal. He contents himself in the course of his annual seaside holiday with at most a dozen pebbles, chosen on account of their rarity, complexity of structure, beauty of colouring or veining, crystalline lustre, fossilized contents or of other qualities which readers of this book may learn to look for in their quest for stones that are worthy of a place in the cabinet.

It is astonishing how few there are who roam the many lovely beaches of this island in search of such pebbles. Yet there must be untold thousands who spend their holiday hours on the beach looking at, handling, and often throwing, pebbles. Of this multitude there are doubtless many who would like to know how the pebbles came to be there, how to name them and how to account for their differences in shape, texture, composition and colour. If they seek for guidance, they find none. The scientific jargon of the geological textbook repels them and it either makes no reference to pebbles at all or does so in the most incidental fashion. Several excellent books on geology for the layman, written in simple language, have appeared in recent years, but, by reason of their brevity, they contain little or no information on this subject. In the effort to make good that lack this book has been written.

In the early and middle years of last century there was a cult of pebble-collecting in vogue among people of means and leisure who stayed at the then rising and fashionable resorts such as Brighton and Scarborough. It so happened that these places possessed beaches of unusually good pebbles, including some that could be classed as semi-precious stones. It was probably cupidity rather than any marked interest in geology that actuated their exploration of the beds of shingle. They combed the beaches with painstaking zeal, employed local lapidaries to cut and polish their finds and compiled glittering collections. It may be that they were too zealous, as they have left little, especially at Brighton, for later generations of enthusiasts. The practice continues, however, but with much less intensity, on several English beaches. It is hoped that this book will help those who still hunt for pebbles of semi-precious stone to know more about their origin and nature. It contains a chapter designed to fulfil this purpose, but we cannot stress too strongly the desirability of cultivating an interest beyond those narrow limits and of gaining a knowledge of pebbles in general.

Pebble-hunting is a pleasant and health-giving hobby, whether pursued on the beach, the lake-side or the river-bank, and all but those who are nearing the last stages of decrepitude can enjoy it. With understanding will come still greater enjoyment. To all who engage in this fascinating quest the author wishes good hunting, an insatiable curiosity and an ever-widening knowledge.

I

THE SHINGLE BEACH

How it was formed and why it is constantly changing. Nature's method of smoothing, shaping and grading the pebbles

What is a pebble? Like all other familiar objects known to man it is easily recognized but not easily defined. The usual dictionary definition, 'a small stone rounded by the action of water', has the merit of conciseness and is fairly accurate, but not every pebble has been rounded by water action and there is some disagreement among the authorities upon the degree of smallness which a rounded stone must attain before it can be classed as a pebble. Some maintain that a pebble can vary in size from a maximum of six inches in its longest diameter to a minimum of $\frac{1}{4}$ inch, the breadth of a pea, while others would accept a much larger range: from a rounded boulder to a minute stone little larger than a grain of sand.

Then there is the question of the stage of rounding which a stone must have reached before it can be regarded as a pebble. That question will always be unanswerable because there is an infinite number of gradations between the jagged fragment of rock and the smoothly rounded pebble and it is impossible to fix upon one point in the long process of shaping and smoothing as a clear division between a rock fragment and a pebble.

So we must content ourselves with the short and simple dictionary definition and assume that every one of the stones on a shingle beach is a pebble, complete or in the making.

The shingle beach is a familiar sight to all who dwell upon or visit the coast of this island. There are few stretches of our coast without one. Indeed, we find shingle everywhere except on the mud flats of expansive estuaries, on beaches consisting wholly of sand, and in places where the sea, even at low water, does not recede from the cliffs.

To understand how pebbles come into existence in such vast numbers, by what means they are shaped and smoothed and how they come to be graded in orderly fashion, from large to small, on the beach, we must consider in some detail the formation of beds of shingle.

Firstly we must always bear in mind that a pebble is a transient thing. It is in the half-way stage of a long existence. Beginning as a fragment of rock, which itself is millions of years old, it ends its existence by being pounded into minute particles or grains. Similarly, the shingle beach which consists entirely of pebbles, is also transient, for it is constantly being moved along the shore by the action of waves. There are beaches, of course, which have large beds of shingle above high-water mark that appear to be permanent enough to harbour vegetation in the narrow spaces among the pebbles. Such shingle, however, must have been hurled upon the beach in gales of exceptional severity. It only awaits another severe gale to be dispersed in its turn.

Secondly, the shingle bed is fairly shallow. It lies on a base far more permanent than itself, usually a shelf or platform of solid rock. The sea cut out, or wore down, this platform when, long ago, it eroded the land on which the beach now stands: the resulting debris then formed the bed of shingle. The sea continued its attack upon the retreating cliffs, from which additional layers of debris came and still ceaselessly come.

Thirdly, with these two points in mind, we may assume that much of the shingle on a normal beach consists of fragments of the local stone torn originally from the cliffs that have long disappeared, and later from the cliffs that are still being eroded. But it would be rash to assume that this is true of all beaches. The effect of incoming and outgoing waves is to move pebbles along the shore at a rate which naturally varies with the strength of the wind, the force of the breakers and the slope of the beach. The rate, even in comparatively calm weather, is far from negligible. Consequently there is a steady drift of shingle along the shore. A beach in a deeply-cut cove enjoys a large measure of immunity from drift, while one on a coast not heavily indented suffers considerable drift. A headland jutting far into the sea on that side of the beach from which drift usually progresses acts as a barrier against it. It will hold up the migration of the shingle for a very long period, but eventually a storm will force some shingle round the corner and bring to the sheltered bay its quota of pebbles from distant beaches. The shape of the coastline will, therefore, be some guide to us in deciding whether the bulk of the shingle on a beach comes from the land that it fringes.

And now to consider in more detail the effects of wave action. Learned men have spent years in observing the behaviour of waves and have written abstruse mathematical treatises about them. These need not concern us, but we must understand the rudiments of wave action in order to appreciate its effects upon the movement, the shaping and the smoothing of pebbles.

Wind produces waves. It beats up the little undulations on the surface of calm water into waves. They then travel forward in the direction in which the wind is blowing. This appears to be so obvious as to be hardly worth mentioning, but it is not so simple as that. Although it is true that wind-driven waves travel forward, it is only the shape of the wave that travels in deep water; its substance remains almost stationary. The explanation of this is that every drop of water in a wave not near the beach revolves in a vertical circle, the drops on the crest of the wave moving forwards and those in the trough of the wave moving backwards. The water immediately in front then takes the shape of the wave, and so on, until the wave breaks near the beach. The breaking wave has travelled far, but the water of which it is composed has scarcely travelled at all.

15

If you desire proof of this you have only to throw out a small piece of wood from the beach beyond the breaking waves and you will at once observe that the crest of the wave carries it forward and the trough draws it back. Or, stand near a field of grown wheat on a windy day. Waves appear to pass right across the field, yet the corn remains rooted. The wave-motion in the cornfield closely resembles that of the sea.

Remembering this, we can now consider the effect upon the beach material of the incoming and breaking waves. From the very moment when the wave breaks it ceases, of course, to be a moving 'shape' and the mass of water rushes up the beach upon which, as we shall see later, it acts either constructively or destructively.

It will be helpful at this stage to grasp and to remember the meaning of three technical terms in use by those who study wave movements. They are 'swash', 'backwash' and 'fetch'. The swash is the rushing water driven up the beach when the wave breaks. The backwash is precisely the opposite and, as its name suggests, is the water returning down the beach after the swash has spent its force. Just as the swash decreases in speed and force as it makes its way up the slope of the beach, so the backwash increases in speed and force as it rushes down. It naturally follows that if the beach has a gentle slope the swash will travel farther and act more powerfully, but if the slope is steep the backwash will be swifter and stronger. Therefore the swash will tend to push pebbles up a gently sloping beach, making it gradually steeper until at last it becomes steep enough for the backwash to become the more energetic and to drag the material down again, eventually making the slope gentle once more. The process can continue indefinitely.

Fetch is the length of the stretch of wind-swept water over which waves travel. The longer the fetch the larger the waves. Such waves, therefore, carry more material up and down the slope of the beach, and so the parts of our coast that lie open to extensive seas are subject to fiercer and more sustained attacks than those which look out upon comparatively narrow stretches of water. For example, the south-west coast bears the brunt of the long Atlantic rollers which have a fetch extending far beyond the south of Ireland, and our East Coast is washed by the North Sea waves with a fetch as far away as the coast of Norway. The beaches of Kent and those of south-west Scotland, on the other hand, enjoy some immunity from far-fetched waves, the Continent being so near to the former and Ireland to the latter. Even where stronger winds blow over those narrow waters they produce smaller waves than moderate winds raise over an expansive fetch. The comparison breaks down, of course, when the narrow seas are lashed by local storms, but in all other conditions it holds good.

If you stand on an open beach—that is, one not enclosed in a bay—and observe the incoming waves on any day when there is neither a flat calm nor a raging storm, you will almost certainly notice that the line of the waves is not entirely parallel with that of the coast. In other words, the waves approach the shore obliquely. They do so because the wind that predominates over their fetch rarely blows at right angles to the shore, and so the waves come in at an acuter angle than one of ninety degrees. Figure 1 will demonstrate this more clearly than any verbal des-

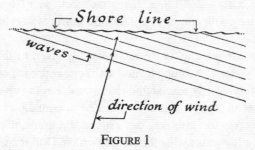

FIGURE 1

cription. As the waves break, their swash reaches up the beach carrying shingle and other material before them. But, because the swash comes in obliquely it will run obliquely up the beach and so will the shingle that it carries. After the swash has reached its limit, the backwash takes command and rushes down the slope of the beach, also bearing shingle with it. The backwash, however,

17

returns by the shortest possible route, that is, straight down the beach. Figure 2 should make these movements plain.

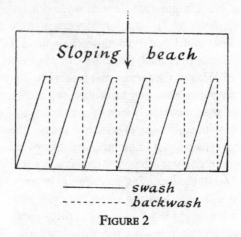

swash
backwash

FIGURE 2

With almost every rising tide this process goes on. The steady inrush and outrush of water along the lines of these right-angled triangles transports the shingle, not merely up and down the beach, but along it. It is for this reason that we have described the shingle beach as a transient thing, for some portions of it are being moved along with almost every tide and nearly always in the same direction.

'Longshore drifting' is the name usually given to this shifting of beach material resulting from the oblique approach of waves to the shore. It is fairly regular and rhythmical, but the up-and-down movement of shingle can sometimes be spasmodic and violent. Storm waves, for instance, can reduce the gradient of a steep beach in a few hours. One terrific gale on the Dorset coast in 1852 altered the gradient of the famous Chesil Beach from about 1 in 4 to about 1 in 9 and shifted a huge mass of pebbles up the beach to form a conspicuous ridge, traces of which are still discernible after more than a century. But storm waves are not the only kind that alter the contours of a beach. Long observation of wave behaviour has shown that in fair weather most waves tend to build up the beach while others tend to drag it back. The former are, therefore, termed constructive waves and the latter destructive. The factor which determines whether a wave is constructive or destructive is the rapidity of wave-succession. If they break at the rate of about six to eight per minute with fair regularity, there is time for the backwash of one wave to recede before the swash of its successor rushes forward. These are the constructive waves. They push more shingle up the beach than they drag back down it. But if the frequency is greater, the breaking wave, receiving the thrust of its predecessor's backwash, plunges down more vertically. Its swash is consequently more feeble and its backwash more powerful so it pulls more material back than it pushes forward. It is, therefore, called a destructive wave.

Here and there we must have noticed that the shingle bed has a scalloped edge along the margin nearest to the sea.

FIGURE 3

The curved ridges of pebbles are highest on the landward side and taper down towards the sea. The little bays usually vary more in depth than in width. The most feasible explanation is that cross-winds have been at work, producing the crossing of waves near the beach. The resulting swash does not flow in the usual long line up the beach but comes up in protruding tongues, making a series of indentations among the bed of small pebbles and the little bays broaden and deepen as the process goes on.

We must now examine the shingle itself and see how the sea has graded the pebbles. Many people are astonished to find that on most beaches they visit the biggest pebbles are at the top of the beach, the smallest near the bottom and, in between, those of intermediate grade. The explanation is simple. Firstly, the bigger stones offer a greater purchase to the incoming waves which can thus push them farther up the beach. Secondly, unless the beach

19

has a steep slope, the swash is more powerful than the backwash. Before the backwash can exert a powerful pull, much of its volume of water will have sunk down into the bed of shingle over which the swash has flowed. The swash started with the impetus of the breaking wave, but the backwash begins the return journey down the beach with no impetus at all. The result is a grading of the pebbles by the tides, from the large stones approaching the size of boulders at the top of the beach, down through all the intermediate stages to the very little pebbles that appear to constitute a bed of gravel at the bottom of the beach. Below them again the sand stretches out beneath the water.

One heavy storm, of course, can upset this symmetrical array. It can flatten the slope of the beach, disperse the large pebbles at the top and drag them back in the powerful backwash of its waves. A large storm wave loses a smaller proportion of its volume of water in the sand and shingle when its backwash rushes down the beach and so it has more dragging power than a normal wave.

Even in long periods of tranquillity the pattern of the beach can vary, often from day to day, as the result of longshore drifting, a change in wind direction, ground swell or exceptionally high tide. Thus, for example, the belt of pebbles of intermediate grade may shrink or expand in width over a week-end.

But enough of the beach in general. Let us look more closely at the pebbles themselves.

If one were to devote a whole lifetime to the scrutinizing of pebbles one would be very lucky indeed to find two of them exactly alike, for, if they were identical in shape, they would almost certainly differ in texture, colour, surface pattern, degree of hardness or the nature of the rocks from which they originated. Various causes combine to give them their form: the nature of the parent rock, the original shape of the rock fragment from which the pebble has been shaped and ground down, the degree of hardness of that rock, the nature of the minerals it contains, its veining and jointing, the amount of material in it that is subject to decomposition or solubility, the position that the pebble occupied on the beach when it first began to be rubbed down by the scraping of other pebbles against it and the means by which it was transported (waves, currents, rivers, glaciers, etc.) to its present position.

As to their shape, pebbles fall into three groups, but between the first and the second, and between the second and the third, there is an infinite number of gradations:

1. SPHERES. In this class we include all those that are only approximately spherical, for a pebble that is a perfect sphere must be a rare find indeed. This is the smallest of the three classes, as the chances of a pebble being scraped and rubbed down uniformly on every part of its surface are slender and, even if the chances were greater, it would have to consist throughout of entirely homogeneous material with no joints, veins or fissures before it could attain this shape. A pebble consisting wholly of fine, hard grains, all of which can put up the same measure of resistance to scrapes, rubs and bumps coming from all directions, is likely to come within this class. Spherical pebbles are more common on beaches that are frequently swept by rough seas than in sheltered coves. Good examples are stones of homogeneous material that have been whirled continuously around, one against another, in river pot-holes.

2. OVOIDS. This is a much larger class. The word 'ovoid' means egg-shaped. As conditions are generally against the attainment of spherical form, it is but natural that the daily rolling to and fro of a beach pebble should make it egg-shaped. We may include in this group those of a much rarer shape—the cylinders. They are much longer than they are broad and have rounded ends. Probably they originated as fragments of a rock that tended to splinter upon being broken.

3. FLATTENED OVOIDS, or oval discs. Again a large class. It is fairly safe to assume that nearly all pebbles of this shape come from laminated rocks—that is to say, rocks made up of thin plates or layers. These plates all run in one direction and the stone can be cleft in that direction only. A common example of a laminated rock is slate. When a slate pebble is worn down by rubbing, it

naturally assumes a flattened form. The rubbing also rounds off its sides. The outcome is a flattened ovoid. The spheres and ovoids are rolled along the beach by the tides, but the flattened ovoids are pushed to and fro. Spherical pebbles on sheltered beaches are comparatively few because the backwash rolls pebbles of that shape more easily than it can drag back flattened ovoids. The former are rolled back into deeper water; the latter are pushed up and down the beach.

From the above we can arrive at one important conclusion: the determining factor in the shaping of most pebbles by wave action is their texture—that is, the disposition of their constituent parts and the material of which they are made. The waves do the rolling, pushing, grinding, rounding and smoothing, but the material and texture of the pebble govern its form.

There are occasional exceptions. For instance, a pebble wedged in the underside of a glacier can have its protruding portion completely filed away. In the next chapter we shall see that glaciers have carried many pebbles to our beaches. Then, again, sand constantly passing over a pebble that has become firmly fixed in a river-bed can wear its upper surface down flat. Driven sand has a filing power that is astonishing. A not uncommon sight on our beaches is a line of sand-dunes at the back of the bed of shingle. Sand-dunes consist of extremely fine grains which, in strong winds, produce a natural sand-blast, and this, in course of time, can file the pebbles down and give them curiously contorted shapes.

Though shingle is present on most of our beaches, there are some shingle beds that are specially noteworthy and that provide exceptionally good opportunities for the study of beach formation and movement.

Foremost of these is Chesil Beach, once described as the 'most extensive and most extraordinary accumulation of shingle in the world'. It may not be the most extensive in the world but in other ways it is probably unique. Civil engineers, geographers, geologists and geomorphologists have contributed articles to learned journals about it, while many non-technical writers have described it in rapturous and romantic terms.

The beach runs south-east along the Dorset coast from Bridport to the Isle of Portland, an uninterrupted stretch of 18 miles. The Isle of Portland, jutting 2½ miles out to sea, acts as a natural groyne and impedes the shifting of the shingle to the east. Chesil Beach is not a beach in the usual sense of that term because, in its last 10 miles, from near Abbotsbury to the Isle of Portland, it is a ridge of shingle with water on both sides, the sea on the south-west side and a lagoon called the Fleet on the north-east for most of the way. Beyond the lagoon the shingle ridge proceeds seawards and links up the Isle of Portland with the mainland. Both its width and its height increase in its last 10 miles between Abbots-bury and the Isle. At the former it is 170 yards wide and 23 feet high and at the latter 200 yards wide and 43 feet high.

Chesil Beach possesses several striking and fascinating features:

1. Its pebbles, particularly those on its seaward side, are graded with an accuracy that is astonishing. They increase steadily and uniformly in size all the way from Bridport to the Isle of Portland, ranging from tiny pellets the size of a pea at the former to stones of 5 or 6 inches in diameter at the latter. It has been stated that, if a blind man who had known the beach from boyhood were taken in a boat to any part of it, he would only have to pick up one pebble to know precisely on what part of the beach he stood. Experiments with broken bricks have proved how inevitably and accurately the process of sorting goes on. Pieces of brick were chosen because they are easily distinguishable from the shingle. They were placed on the beach at various points between high- and low-water mark. Every one of them in due course made its way to its appropriate place on the ridge and lay side by side with pebbles of the same magnitude.

The inference to be drawn from these experiments is that long-shore drifting by wave action is responsible. But if that is so, why does not longshore drifting produce equally precise sorting on other long stretches of shingle? So far there has been no complete answer to that question. Further prolonged and detailed study of wave action may provide one.

2. Equally extraordinary, if not more so, is the behaviour of the pebbles below low-water mark on the seaward side of the beach. As they are always submerged they are almost hidden from view, but it is apparent from all the observations made of them and their movements, that they are also graded, but in the opposite direction! Evidence of the truth of this is not entirely complete. A long series of diving operations would be necessary to confirm it. Various theories have been advanced in explanation of the phenomenon, but a completely convincing one has yet to be put forward.

3. Nine-tenths of all the pebbles are flint. This in itself is not surprising, as flint-bearing cliffs of chalk lie to the west at intervals between Seaton and Sidmouth, but their contribution to Chesil Beach seems to be out of all proportion to their extent. It is possible that those cliffs are the remnants of a huge mass of chalk that was eroded by the sea ages ago and now lies beneath its surface and that the flints it bore have been subsequently dragged by tidal action eastwards to form the beach. Pebbles of limestone and chert, a stone that resembles flint, form the bulk of the deposit at the Isle of Portland end. The rest of the shingle consists of beautiful quartzite pebbles from Budleigh Salterton; jasper, carried to the sea by the river Otter; granite from Cornwall and some pebbles that were originally fragments of rock entirely foreign to the south-west coast. We shall consider in the next chapter the journeyings of pebbles over great distances.

Another impressive stretch of shingle, one of the finest in Britain, is on the Suffolk coast. It extends for 11 miles from the pleasant seaside resort, Aldeburgh, in the north, to the appropriately named Shingle Street, in the south. All this long beach consists of shingle only. Sand is barely visible. One of its curious features is that it presents an insurmountable barrier to the river Alde in its efforts to reach the sea. The river comes within about 50 yards of the sea south of Aldeburgh but is held back by the bank of shingle and runs behind it until the shingle peters out at North Weir Point, 11 miles to the south-west. There the frustrated river at last flows out to sea. Nearly half-way between Aldeburgh and North Weir Point the coast rather sharply alters its southerly course and turns to the south-west. The corner or foreland thus formed is shown on maps as Orford Ness, but the Ness is really the whole 11-mile stretch of shingle. On this coast longshore drifting proceeds southwards, as the waves are driven in by the dominant winds from the north-east. The shingle ridge has consequently extended itself gradually in that direction. There is evidence that it grew in the 700 years ending in 1897 about 5½ miles, or 13–14 yards every year. It suffered a setback in 1897, when a violent storm shortened it by a mile, but it has since renewed its advance.

Orford Ness displays another interesting feature, which is to be seen in a few other large deposits of shingle. At the foreland the shingle is deeply furrowed, giving the impression that a gigantic plough has been at work upon it. The ridges and hollows are roughly parallel with one another, the former being known as 'fulls' and the latter as 'swales'. South of the foreland they run along the shingle bank for several miles. Each of the fulls probably represents a stage in the growth of the shingle bank, or 'spit', as it is technically termed. The popular conception of a spit is a narrow ridge of sand projecting seawards or running parallel with the beach. There can be spits, however, consisting entirely of shingle and, of these, Orford Ness is the outstanding example.

Large stretches of furrowed shingle can be seen on two other parts of the coast. East of Eastbourne, in Sussex, is the extensive pebble beach known as the Crumbles. At one part it is furrowed into 60 fulls, all running parallel with the sea, some of them being more than a mile long. Walking north-eastwards along the beach from Eastbourne towards Pevensey, one becomes aware that there has been some grading of the pebbles, for they tend to become smaller as one proceeds.

Going much farther east, we come to Dungeness, lying between

Rye and Hythe on the Cinque Ports coastline. On that coast are spread out the greatest stretches of shingle in this country. The term 'ness' is derived from an Anglo-Saxon word meaning nose. Dungeness, one mass of shingle, is a nose pointing out into the sea. This famous foreland has been the subject of a considerable literature and numerous experts have tried to elucidate its complex structure. One coast of the ness, or nose, faces south, the other east. Waves driven up the Channel from the west meet the former obliquely and cause longshore drifting towards the tip of the nose. The shingle which is eventually driven around that point is thrown up on the east coast of the ness by waves blown thither by north-east winds. The fact that the tip of the nose continues sharp is thought to be due to the short distance between it and the French coast, towards which it directly points, as waves travelling straight across from France to the nose have insufficient space in which to become destructively large.

The furrows of the Dungeness shingle span its whole breadth. These appear to be innumerable fulls and swales lying parallel to its east coast. Those running into the centre of the ness and on to its southern shore are arranged in a more complicated pattern. The probability is that every one of them marks the boundary between sea and shore at one stage or another of the building up of the ness.

Almost all its pebbles are of flint. The few interlopers are of sandstone and quartzite, some of which have travelled far.

We must defer discussion of the many other fascinating shingle beaches on our coastline to Chapter V, where we shall make a tour of the beaches of England and Wales in search of pebbles of unusual interest. Meanwhile two kinds of shingle beach that are not sea-washed at all deserve our scrutiny. They are raised beaches and lake shores.

1. RAISED BEACHES. Around the coastline of the British Isles, but elevated some distance above it, are beaches that the sea has deserted long ago. Some of them have not felt its impact for centuries, some for thousands and some for millions of years. How

has this come about? Well, clearly, either the land must have risen or the level of the sea must have declined since the formation of the beach. Both these changes and their opposites have occurred, not once but many times. Here and there along our coast traces of tree-stumps near low-water mark prove that either the water level has risen or the land has suffered depression, while the existence of raised beaches demonstrates the reverse of both these alternatives. There is geological evidence that, on the whole, it has been the variation in the sea level rather than that of the land which has raised the beaches and submerged the forests. The process is still going on, though almost imperceptibly. For example, part of the Swedish coast, on the Gulf of Bothnia, rose 19½ inches during the last century and is still rising. Our own south-east coast, on the other hand, is losing height relative to that of the sea, but so gradually that the rate of decline cannot be measured with complete accuracy; it is estimated at less than ⅛-inch per annum.

Raised beaches and submerged forests can be found on the same piece of coast, the raising and the lowering having occurred at different times. In most cases the submergence took place after the elevation, so the original elevation must have been that much higher.

The major cause of the relative changes in the height of land and sea was the enormous expansion of the polar ice-cap about one million years ago and the consequent spreading of huge sheets of ice over large areas of Europe, North America and much of the intervening seas. As we shall have to consider the Ice Age in more detail in the next chapter, when discussing the journeys made by pebbles, a summary of its effects upon land and sea levels will suffice here.

(a) To produce these thousands of square miles of thick ice an incalculable amount of water was necessary. Where did it all come from? Obviously, nearly all of it must have been drawn from the sea by evaporation. The result of this loss of water was a drop of some hundreds of feet in sea level all over the globe.

Beaches previously formed along the coastline were left high and dry.

(b) Then the terrific weight of the massive sheets upon so large a part of the earth's surface would subject the outer crust to a severe strain and depress the surface. The depression would not be uniform. It would be much more severe in some areas than in others, but the general effect would be to restore to some extent the difference in the relative levels of land and sea caused by (a).

(c) Finally, with the melting of all the ice comes a universal rise in sea level, followed more slowly by a rise in the depressed land level.

In our part of the world there have been no violent fluctuations in the relative levels of sea and land since the effects of the final melting of the ice wore away, and that was about 10,000 years ago. The sea then began to build new beaches on our coasts at a level not greatly different from the present one.

It has for long been customary to classify the raised beaches of Great Britain into three grades to which the terms '25-foot beach', '50-foot beach', and '100-foot beach', are applied, but this is an over-simplification, as in all three classes there is considerable variation in height. In searching for these deposits we must realize that, in the ages that have elapsed since the sea built them up, vegetation has overgrown and now completely obscured many of them. The towns of Dundee and Greenock have been built upon such beaches.

Here are a few which still preserve the character of beds of shingle: Brighton provides an excellent example of one, 30 feet above the sea-washed shingle; at Portland Bill there is a notable one of 65 feet in height; one of 20 feet is at Hope's Nose near Torquay; at St. Ives in Cornwall, Barnstaple Bay in Devonshire, near Weston-super-Mare, at St. Helen's in the Isle of Wight, and on the Gower Peninsula in South Wales are other noteworthy examples. But Scotland has the most numerous and most impressive raised beaches, some of them consisting of large spreads of shingle. They range in height above present sea level from 10 to about 100 feet. The greater concentration of massive glaciers there in the Ice Age, and the heavier strain they exerted upon the land surface, probably account for the number and height of the Scottish raised beaches.

2. LAKE SHORES. Lakes, even small ones, have their beaches. Winds disturb their surface and produce little waves which roll small stones up and down the lake's marginal strip of sloping land. But a lake is landlocked and has no tides, so the rolling of pebbles to and fro is insignificant in comparison with the effects of sea-wave action. The great grinding mill to be seen at work on the sea beach is scarcely noticeable at the lake-side. There are, of course, enormous lakes in other parts of the world which have so large a 'fetch' that their pebbles are transported along their shores by wave-driven winds and are, in course of time, shaped and smoothed. Lake Michigan, for instance, shows ample evidence of the capacity of a landlocked and non-tidal expanse of water to produce longshore drifting of beach material.

It follows from this that the waves on the surface of a British lake take a much longer time to convert a rock fragment into a pebble. Yet one finds on the shores of many of our small lakes well-fashioned and beautifully-smoothed pebbles. The lake, however, is not entirely responsible for the production of all of them. One of several other agencies than lake waves could have rubbed them into pebble form. Here are two possible ones:

(a) Giant glaciers in the Ice Age scooped up the hollows in the gravel which later became filled with water and which now form the basins of many of our lakes. The pebbles, gathered up by the glacier in its journey, and already fully shaped and smoothed, fell into the lake basin when the ice melted.

(b) We usually find that a lake is fed by a river or by mountain streams. They could have carried small stones over a long distance. On the journey those stones, bumping and rubbing against others in the river-bed, would have assumed the form of pebbles before they reached the lake. The process of rubbing and shaping would then slow down very considerably but it would go on, the little wind-waves gently moving the pebbles, perhaps no more than a fraction of an inch in the course of a day.

Naturally, we expect to find that nearly all the pebbles on a lake beach are composed of the same material as the local rock. Those that are not must have been carried to the lake by the action of glaciers or rivers; if by the latter they will probably be made of one or other of the rocks of the region through which the river has flowed; if by the former they may originally have been pieces of a rock hundreds or even thousands of miles away.

Many people are bewildered when they come upon pebbles at the top of a hill far from the coast. Can it be, they ask, that the sea once covered the land to such a depth? That possibility must not be ruled out altogether, because there have been some astonishing vertical movements of the earth's surface in the course of geological time. The British Isles lay under the water in the Cambrian Age, between four and five hundred million years ago, and did not completely emerge from the sea until that immense span of time was nearing its end. Nevertheless, so much of the surface has been subsequently worn away by weathering action that the chances of our finding any traces of a *sea* beach on a hilltop far from the coast are remote.

River pebbles still abound on high ground above the river that shaped them, because the river has cut deeper and deeper into its valley and has greatly lowered its bed. The Thames, for instance, eroded its valley at one period to a depth of 80 feet and river pebbles, rounded by the Thames thousands of years ago, have been found on the 100-foot contour line. Yet that height is insignificant in comparison with the distances to which glaciers have raised pebbles. One extraordinary example of glacier-borne pebbles transported inland to a great height is to be seen on the slopes of Moel Tryfan, a mountain in Snowdonia. There the pebbles lie 1,400 feet above sea level. The glacier which bore them had scraped them up from the floor of the Irish Sea into the heart of Snowdonia and deposited them there when it melted. So it is not very surprising after all to discover pebbles on a hilltop. If there are traces of glacial action in the vicinity you may be fairly certain that ice was the agent that brought the pebbles up the hill and left them there. One of the delights of the pebble-seeker is to discover the objects of his search in the least likely places and to determine whence and by what means they came to be there.

II

THE BIRTH, LIFE AND DEATH
OF A PEBBLE

*Its journeys through time and space. The strangers to
the beach: river-borne and ice-borne pebbles*

A pebble begins its life as a rock fragment that has become detached from the parent rock by some natural agency. The usual cause is the battering of the shore cliffs by rough seas, but the sea is not responsible for all the damage. The weather, very slowly but very surely, breaks down even the hardest rock. Sun, wind and rain gradually etch its surface. Water, freezing in the crannies of the rock, exerts a powerful leverage and, in the course of many years, splits it ever more widely and deeply, while vegetation, rooting in the split surface, contributes to the slow disintegration.

Let us briefly consider the process of rock erosion by the sea on a beach backed by cliffs. Day in and day out the waves batter the base of the cliffs, gradually and steadily undercutting them. The smallest cracks in the rock aid the destructive effect of the water, as the inrush suddenly compresses the air in the cleft and the outrush suddenly releases it. Thus the cracks are widened and the explosive force becomes all the greater. At last the undercutting brings down part of the face of the cliff with a rush and a pile of broken rocks lies at the bottom of the cliffs. For a time this heap of debris acts as a defensive barrier against the incoming waves, but once the sea has begun to level it down, the broken rocks help in the attack. They are a supply of ammunition with which the waves can increase their battering force. The pace of erosion is quickened as the process of undercutting is resumed.

The waves have other supplies of ammunition at hand. In rough weather the beach pebbles take a share in the bombardment. Even the submerged rocks below the low-water mark can help the attack. On a shallow shore the waves break some distance out from the beach. They scour the bottom, wrench out stones embedded in the sand, wear down the rocks that outcrop from it and carry all this eroded material forward. Some of it is sharp-edged, like the fragments that have fallen from the cliff-face, and causes a particularly destructive impact. The mass of fragments that fall to the beach by wave erosion or weathering grows ever greater and the first stage in the life of the pebbles is over.

Then begins the long, slow process of converting the jagged, angular fragment of rock into the smooth and fairly round pebble of the shingle beach. We have seen in the preceding chapter how the recurring tides, day after day, year after year, and century after century, roll the stones of the beach, one against another, with endless and remorseless regularity, grinding and smoothing them and even sorting them in accordance with their size. How long does this process take? It is impossible to estimate it with any accuracy, because rocks vary so much in their degree of hardness and other circumstances, which we will consider later, have to be taken into account. If the beach cliffs consist of a very hard compact rock such as basalt, which is of volcanic origin, they will not only stand up to the onslaught of the waves more sturdily than softer rocks but also resist more stoutly the weathering action of sun, wind and rain. And when at last disintegration begins, the rock fragments withstand far more tenaciously the efforts of the waves to grind and smooth them. But if the sea cliffs are of sandstone, the process is much shorter, for only the most compact sandstone is tough enough to maintain a very long struggle against both weather and tide. Indeed, a pebble of soft sandstone would be ground down to nothing long before wave action could rub a single corner off a fragment of basalt.

Sandstone is a striking example of a life-cycle ending as it began and is, therefore, comparable to the 'dust to dust' cycle of man. The sand grains of which it is composed may have been laid down hundreds of millions of years ago at the bottom of some sea or lake which subsequently disappeared. The grains meanwhile had become a compact mass through being held together by a cementing material, either silica or iron oxide. Then, as we have seen, the fragment of sandstone is broken off the sandstone cliff, becomes in course of time a pebble and, as it is rubbed down by the waves, resolves itself at last into the separate grains of which it was composed. If this earth lasts for millions of years again, the cycle may repeat itself.

Perhaps the greatest of contrasts is to be found in the pebbles that are formed out of chalk cliffs; the 'White Cliffs of Dover' and the chalk of the Yorkshire coast. The chalk contains numerous nodules of flint. It is comparatively soft and is easily crumbled, but flint is hard and unyielding. The shingle resulting from the wearing down of the cliffs is, therefore, rich in flint pebbles, very durable and very attractive, but the chalk that had held them in its embrace for some scores of millions of years has a much shorter life once it has been torn from the cliff and become a fragment on the beach.

If you walk along any of the beaches that lie below the white cliffs of chalk you will notice that many of the flint nodules have not had their corners completely rounded off. They are still to some extent angular and have yet to be shaped by wave action into the mature beach pebble. You will rightly conclude that the hard flint is strenuously resisting the efforts of the waves to grind and shape it. Unlike the sandstone and the limestone pebble, the lump of flint is not composed of tiny fragments. It is a solid mass of unyielding silica. In time, however, the rubbing and grinding process will shape it into a fairly round pebble; it will become smaller and smaller and will at last disappear. The minute fragments into which it has been filed down will become sand grains and will join the uncountable millions of grains that form the sands of the sea. These vast stretches which, it has been computed, form a border to nine-tenths of the coastline of the world, are a colossal pebble cemetery, for much of them consists of pulverized pebbles. A sand beach that has been formed by the breaking down of flint pebbles and of other stones comprised of silica, such as quartz, is said to consist of 'sharp' sand. It is so called because the grains are angular and some of their edges are sharp. Why is it that the pebbles of which they once formed a part were rounded, but the grains are sharp-edged and angular? That was their shape when they were broken off the parent pebble and they have kept it because an extremely thin film of sea water separates one grain from another, preventing them from rubbing one another down.

But even sand is not the ultimate stage in the lingering death of a pebble. The last is the conversion of sand into silt. The minute particles that make up a deposit of silt are very much finer than the smallest sand-grains. When the deposit is very thick the upper layers press heavily upon the lower layers and consolidate them gradually into stone. Many of the rocks of this country have originated in this way. One of the commonest is shale and we shall encounter many shale pebbles in our beach wanderings. The life-cycle of a shale pebble is mud–shale–mud, for beginning as mud, it becomes shale in the course of ages and is then slowly worn down again through the centuries into the fine particles that help to make up a deposit of mud.

So far we have been considering only those pebbles which originated as rock fragments torn from the sea cliffs, but every beach contains pebbles which have reached it by a longer route and we must now give them some attention. It would be substantially true to say that the sea cliffs or, in the absence of cliffs, the land adjacent to the shore, contributes by far the highest proportion of pebbles to all of our beaches, but the other contributory sources supply a share by no means small or unimportant. The study of beach pebbles would be very much easier and very much less fascinating, if all of them were derived from the land at the back of the beach, because all we should then have to do would be to determine the nature of the local rock and we should at once be able to name every pebble on that beach. The task of identification would not be quite so light if the local rocks were not all of the same kind. This is not at all unusual. As some rocks are harder than others, the sea makes a greater inroad upon the softer rocks and this is one of the main causes of the indentation of the coastline. Coves and bays mark the successful attacks of the sea upon the softer rocks and so we should expect to find upon the beach a higher proportion of pebbles derived from them.

Some of the pebbles that are not of local origin have not made a long journey, others have travelled some scores of miles, while there may be some that have come hundreds of miles. Let us see how they make these journeys.

Firstly, one important agency in the transportation of pebbles is river action. If a river makes its way to the sea on, or within reasonable distance of, your beach, you may be sure that pebbles drawn from the rocks through which the river has made its course will be present on the beach in fairly large numbers. A river is a very effective pebble-maker. Even a little stream is not to be despised as a pebble source, for the power of running water is astonishing. It carries away so much of the land into the sea as to make one wonder how long it will be before the world's rivers have intermingled land with sea completely. For example, the rivers of the United States of America alone transport annually 800,000,000 tons of rocks and soil into the Atlantic and Pacific oceans. Setting aside the soluble salts that a river carries away in solution, we may say that it transports material in two ways: it carries light and small substances such as sand grains, silt and particles of mud; and these, in a fairly swiftly flowing river, neither float nor sink but are held, so to speak, in suspension; and it also bears along with it larger and heavier material, chiefly stones, dragging them along the bottom. The first of the two is called the suspended load and the latter the traction load, because it is drawn or dragged. The suspended load of sand, silt and mud goes to form the bed of the estuary and to spread itself out on the lowest slopes of the beach, much of it descending below low-water mark. The traction load is an important contributor to the pebbles on the beach. American authorities on river transportation have calculated that the Mississippi carries annually into the Gulf of Mexico a suspended load of 136 million tons and a traction load of 40 million tons. Much of the traction load must consist of rock fragments and pebbles, so we are forced to the conclusion that the beaches of the Gulf of Mexico receive many millions of tons of pebbles every year from the Mississippi.

Our own, much smaller, British rivers make, of course, a much more modest contribution to our beach deposits, but it is a far greater one than is popularly supposed. Let us see how they contrive to be pebble-makers and how the pebbles make their journey to the beach.

A river erodes or eats away its own bed in two directions, downwards and sideways. It drags away material from its bed and from its sides; the steeper the descent of the river, the faster is its flow, and the faster the flow the more material does it hack out from its bed and sides and carry to the sea. Thus a river may be said to be a sculptor of the land surface. In our temperate climate, with its fairly heavy rainfall, the rivers of Britain, though comparatively short, are numerous and generally swift and they are consequently, except during droughts, very busy transportation agents. They are, therefore, said to possess fairly high powers of abrasion. This term, derived directly from the Latin *abradere*, 'to shave off', simply means the power of rubbing away or wearing down. The actual process of the cutting away of material by a river from its bed and sides is called corrasion, from the Latin *corradere*, 'to scrape'. Experts who have devoted themselves to the study of erosion by rivers have computed that the corrasive power of a river varies as the square of its velocity. This formula may bewilder the reader who is not mathematically minded, but the calculation is very simple. Let us suppose that heavy rain has trebled the velocity of a river, and let us consider the effect of that

37

increase of speed upon a rock embedded in it. The number of fragments of stone and other material that now scrape and bump against that rock will be multiplied by 3, and every one of them will strike it with threefold violence. Consequently the corrasive, or scraping, power of the river has increased to $3 \times 3 = 9$ times, or to the square of 3, or—to put the same thing in the way the formula has it—as the ratio of the square of the new velocity to the square of the old.

As for the transporting power (and a moment's thought will enable you to see the difference between that and the corrasive power) the increase is even more startling. Earnest students of the subject have conducted experiments in rivers of many kinds and under diverse conditions and have reached the conclusion that the biggest object that running water can carry varies as the fourth, fifth or sixth power of its velocity. This means that, if the velocity be trebled, it can transport objects at least $3 \times 3 \times 3 \times 3 = 81$ times as large. The trebling of the velocity of a river pouring down a steeper slope than the normal might enable it to carry away objects $3 \times 3 \times 3 \times 3 \times 3 \times 3 = 729$ times as large.

Well, these figures may seem incredible, but we must bear in mind that, in ordinary conditions, a river can roll only small fragments along its bed and that, when the size of these is multiplied by 81 or even by 729, it is not enormous. It becomes enormous only in times of disastrous floods, when rivers burst their banks, alter the whole surface of the countryside and sweep away trees, walls and houses. Our mathematical formulae, which at the best are only very approximate, must then be abandoned, because the river is no longer confined to its bed and has become a wide flood.

And now for the birth and life of the pebble formed in a river-bed and carried to the beach. Let us suppose that the stream, by its corrasive power, has torn away from its bed or its side a fragment of stone. That fragment, as in the case of the piece removed from the sea cliff, will be rough and angular. It will at once sink to the bottom and will remain there until heavy rainfall has raised the speed of the current to the point at which it can move it, or, in more technical language, at which it is capable of bearing a traction load. The fragment bumps its way along, scraping against its fellows, and against other stones embedded below or on either side. The grinding and shaping process has already begun. It could have begun earlier if the river had its source on a mountainside and had dislodged the fragment on its way down to more level ground.

The rain ceases and settled weather sets in. Our infant pebble sinks down again and has an undisturbed life until rain again quickens the river into fresh activity. So the process continues until the pebble reaches the sea to receive its final shaping and smoothing by wave action on the beach. It may, of course, have become a mature pebble before it completed its journey. One of the many deciding factors is, naturally, the length of the river; another is the hardness of the rocks through which it flows and against which it has scraped the pebble, but, of all the agencies which convert the rock fragment into the river pebble, the most potent is the pot-hole.

Here and there in the course of a stream there are eddies in which the water has a whirling motion. The eddy sucks into its centre several jagged fragments of rock. This at once creates a crude drilling machine. The stones caught in the vortex swirl around, scraping one another and deepening the circular hollow in the bed. The pot-hole becomes the perfect pebble factory. In all probability it is the most efficient and rapid of all pebble-makers. Heavy rain will sooner or later raise the speed of the stream and carry away the rounded or partly rounded pebbles on their way to the sea, but, as the velocity decreases, other stones will take their place in the pot-hole to have their corners removed and to be ground down in their turn.

Hence it is clear that a pebble may reach the sea already shaped and smoothed and that this process and the journey downstream may take a comparatively short time. On the other hand, a rock fragment that has not been sucked into an eddy may have to wait for its final conversion into pebble form until the waves that pound it to and fro on the beach have completed their work. Other fragments, borne along by sluggish streams which pursue a meandering course, may take ages to complete their seaward journeys. Some are diverted into quiet backwaters where they may lie undisturbed for countless years until a surging flood hurls them out. So many and so diverse are the circumstances to be taken into account that it is impossible to estimate the average time taken by a piece of rock to travel from the upper reaches of a river to its estuary and thence to join the other pebbles on the beach. All that we know is that under the most favourable conditions it may take a few weeks, while under the least favourable it may take many centuries.

Secondly, another and far more powerful agency in the transportation of pebbles is, or rather has been, ice action. It is necessary to speak in the past tense of the carriage of pebbles by ice because it ceased in all parts of the world thousands of years ago, except in the Arctic and Antarctic regions and among extremely high mountains.

In order to gain a clear understanding of pebble transportation by ice we must give some attention to the effect of the ice ages upon this country. You will note, in the first place, that Britain underwent several ice ages. For many years geologists keenly disputed with one another upon the number and duration of these periods of glaciation, but they have now accumulated enough evidence of the advance and retreat of the vast ice sheets that spread into Europe from the Arctic circle to agree among themselves that there were altogether four ice ages and that, from the first advance of the ice to its last retreat, something like one million years elapsed. It appears, too, that the ice made its final departure from Britain about 10,000 years ago.

We must note also that man had already arrived here, though in an early stage of his evolution, before the first advance of the ice and that he had become *Homo sapiens* before its fourth and last departure. To the geologist, who has a time scale of at least

40

2,000,000,000 years, an event occurring a mere 10,000 years ago is more recent than last month is to the historian.

Another and most extraordinary feature of the ice ages is that between the second and third there was a long and very warm period. Fossils of creatures that lived in Britain at that time reveal the amazing fact that southern mammals, the elephant, the rhinoceros and the hippopotamus, roamed the land and warm-water molluscs inhabited our seas. Altogether the glacial and the inter-glacial periods form so attractive a chapter in the geological history of this country that one is tempted to dwell upon it, but we must confine our attention to the transportation of pebbles by ice.

At the time of maximum glaciation, which was probably the second Ice Age, an enormous sheet of ice covered this country from the far north of Scotland to as far south as a line drawn from the Bristol Channel to the valley of the Thames. The line does not follow the course of the Thames strictly but turns a little northward, misses London and comes out on the East Coast near Harwich. The surface of the country north of this line contains bountiful evidence of ice action.

Many British visitors to the Continent have seen Swiss glaciers. Compared with the glaciers that crunched their way across this country they are utterly insignificant. For instance, the glaciers of Snowdonia were some 1,000 feet thick. The polar ice-cap had spread itself southwards in all directions. A huge sheet of ice stretched from Scandinavia across the North Sea. Like a gigantic bull-dozer the glaciers and ice-sheets tore over the land, ripping all obstacles out of their way, scraping and scouring the rocks and carrying the rock fragments for enormous distances. Many of these fragments were frozen into the body of the glacier and thus enjoyed a comparatively tranquil journey, but others became wedged into the sides and the bottom of the glacier. In this position they provided the moving ice with a set of teeth with which to tear and score the ground. The glacier became a giant file, its rock teeth rasping the surface it traversed. The small glaciers of Switzerland appear to be stationary. They move very slowly indeed, but the great ice-sheets that sculptured the surface of this country moved with some rapidity. Of an incalculable weight, and studded with rock teeth, they broadened and deepened the valleys and levelled undulations in the ground. When the great mass thundered over a surface of rock, the screeching teeth cut furrows in it. The technical term for such furrows is 'striations' (Latin: *stria*, 'a groove'), a word to be remembered, because we shall see in the next chapter that many ice-borne pebbles can be identified by the striations on their surface.

As the Ice Age neared its end, the melting of the vast ice-sheets began, but the earth and rocks they had scooped up on the way could not melt. They were deposited on the ground. Some had travelled short distances; others had been carried for hundreds of miles. It must, therefore, follow that, if you find a piece of rock in an inland region that possesses no rock at all of the kind you have found, you have come upon an instance of ice transportation. That piece of rock had been torn out of its natural setting by the glacier, frozen into it and carried along until rising temperature stopped the ice and melted it. Geologists call large blocks of such rocks 'erratics', because they have erred or wandered from the parent rock. There are innumerable erratics in Great Britain. For example, there are certain kinds of granite in Galloway and Ailsa Craig, in Scotland, that are not to be found in any rock formations in southern Britain, yet erratic blocks of this granite have travelled to Cheshire, Lancashire, North Wales and the Isle of Man. Boulders of a rock peculiar to Merionethshire have been transported to Staffordshire and Warwickshire, while blocks of a Norwegian rock, laurvikite, have travelled in and across the North Sea ice-sheets to the coast of Yorkshire.

The passengers carried by the ice were not only separate pieces of rock. The main load was a mass of debris torn up from the surface of the region traversed by the ice. This debris was a mixture of powdered rock and crumbled soil, a sticky compound, in which innumerable pebbles and boulders were embedded. When the Ice

Age ended, the melting ice-sheets left enormous deposits of this boulder clay, as it is called by geologists. It lies over most of Lowland Scotland, northern and central England and East Anglia, and in some places it is hundreds of feet thick. Consequently, many of our sea cliffs are either capped by it or are wholly made up of it, and so the beaches below them have a ready-made supply of pebbles close to hand.

Among the pebbles on the beach are many that have travelled directly thither as ice passengers. We should naturally expect to find them on the coasts north of the line defining the most southerly advance of the ice. Yet some of them are present in the shingle beds on coasts south of that line. How can this have happened? Well, clearly, a second transporting agency must have been at work. One that we have already considered, river action, could have helped in the later stages of the journey, and one to which we must now give some attention, the transporting of pebbles to, and along, the coast by the tides, could have carried them for even greater distances than the ice.

Thirdly, the movement of pebbles by sea water is the most powerful of all the transporting agencies. A pebble is of relatively lighter weight in water than in air and is more easily moved in salt water than in fresh.

Until very recent years the movement of pebbles along the coast was thought to be due to longshore currents, i.e. currents running roughly parallel to, and near the shore, but patient investigation has proved the action of waves and not of currents to be mainly responsible. Currents are capable of transporting fine sand and silt but not pebbles. On the other hand, if the current is strong enough to be classed as a tidal race, it can easily move small pebbles for long distances, but tidal races off our coasts are not numerous.

On many of our beaches we see that groynes made of stout timber or concrete have been fixed at intervals along the shore at right angles to the incoming waves. This is man's device to maintain the stability of his beaches by hindering the drift of sand and shingle along them. One glance at the beach on either side of one of these groynes enables us to decide the direction of the drift, for the sand or shingle is very much higher on the side against which the drift moves. In the absence of groynes the general configuration of the beach should be a reliable guide, but, if we are in doubt, we must fall back upon our memory of the following little summary of the prevalent direction of drift along the coasts of England and Wales.

(a) Along the south coast it is from west to east.

(b) Along the east coast it is from north to south.

(c) Along the west coast it is from south to north.

There are, alas, exceptions to this as to almost all rules, but they are easy to remember. The important ones are·

1. A large stretch of the Norfolk coast runs E—W. Here the prevailing drift westward of Sheringham is westwards in the direction of the Wash.

2. Much of our heavily indented west coast runs in an easterly direction, e.g. the coast of North Wales. On all these stretches the prevailing drift is eastward.

3. Rule (c) does not apply to that part of the west coast which lies between Walney Island and St. Bees Head. From the latter to the former the drift is southward.

So long as we remember that the three statements (a), (b) and (c), and the three exceptions to them, are for our *general* guidance and that purely local conditions may make them inapplicable to certain beaches, we shall not go far wrong.

Because wind produces waves, and because waves produce the drift of shingle along the shore, we seem to be forced to the conclusion that the direction of the prevailing wind in any part of the coastline will determine the direction of the drift of beach material along it. The argument may be logically sound but is nevertheless misleading. We have to distinguish between winds that are prevalent and winds that are dominant. The latter have much more powerful influence than the former upon the drift of shingle. The prevailing wind along our coasts is from the south-west. It speeds the long Atlantic rollers that approach the Cornish coast from the south of Ireland, and, because it happens to be also the dominant wind, it drives the waves up towards the English Channel and the Irish Sea, causing the eastward drift along the south coast from Land's End to Dover, and the northward drift along the west coast from Land's End to the Solway Firth. But on the east coast, although the south-west wind is the prevailing one, it has little effect on wave action because it blows out to sea from the land. The dominant wind there comes from the north-east over the North Sea, causing the waves of that huge expanse of water to beat from that direction upon the east coast and to make its shingle drift southward.

The transportation of beach material for great distances along the coast is not confined to the shingle that lies between high- and low-water mark. It includes also the submerged material lying below the latter. As on land, there are many outcrops of rock on the sea bottom. The sea very gradually erodes them by scouring them with sand and by dashing fragments of rock against them. It has been proved by the experiments of students of current action that a current flowing in the sea at a higher speed than $2\frac{1}{2}$ feet per second can move fairly large pebbles along the bottom if the bottom is a stretch of sand. We have already noted, however, that fast currents are not very common, so the amount of material transported by their agency is only a fraction of the vast amount moved by the action of waves on the beach. That fraction, however, is far from insignificant. The English Channel, for instance, holds the waste material of the land that once, and not so long ago in geological time, joined this country to the Continent. That huge deposit is an endless source of supply to the shingle beaches of the Channel coast.

Seaweed also makes a small contribution! It attaches itself to under-water pebbles very firmly, grows towards the surface of the water and is helped by the air-vessels it contains, to float. A very familiar sight on most beaches, roughly between high and low-water mark, is dark brown seaweed bearing bladder-like growths.

One of the childish delights of a seaside holiday is to produce little explosions by banging these small bladders between two flat stones. The commoner kinds are called bladder wrack and knotted wrack. In the former the bladders grow in pairs; in the latter the bladders are larger and grow singly. The bladders give great buoyancy to these weeds in the water. The buoyancy and their tenacious hold upon the pebbles to which they have attached themselves help them to drag large stones for long distances.

And now we come to the last of the transporting agencies: man himself. Let us suppose that a ship bound for a British port from Australia takes in ballast before the voyage and that this ballast, as is often the case, consists of shingle. When nearing the home port she is driven shorewards by a gale and breaks up on submerged rocks some little way out to sea. In the course of time she disintegrates. Then, over a much longer period, the shingle is very gradually borne ashore to be distributed over a long stretch of coast. The result is that pebbles from the other side of the globe have made their way to a British beach. If the parent rock from which they were formed in Australia differs in its composition from rock in this country, they will present a problem of no little magnitude to the geologist and the geographer, to say nothing of the amateur pebble-hunter.

Then, again, man builds sea-defences such as breakwaters and sea-walls. He also builds moles, jetties and promenades. If the local stone does not lend itself to the construction of these works because it cannot easily be shaped into rectangular blocks, he transports stone from a distant quarry. Some years pass and then pebbles of that stone are found on the beach. It is, naturally, much easier to determine their origin than to identify the fragment of Australian ballast, but, like all other strangers to the beach, they give the inquiring searcher enough food for thought to make his quest interesting.

Thus we see that the journeys of a pebble through time and space can vary enormously; from a few yards to thousands of miles and from a few months to measureless ages. At the one extreme we have the pebble of soft sandstone, coming into existence as a fragment of the sandstone cliff and being rapidly ground into sand-grains on its own beach by the waves. At the other we have the piece of Norwegian rock borne by ice to our shores many thousands of years ago and still lying there ten thousand years after the melting of the ice.

The cycle goes endlessly and steadily on. The finest grains become compacted into solid rock. Millions of years later the encroaching sea, aided by sun, wind and rain, breaks up the rock. A pebble is born. The waves roll it along the beaches from Cornwall to Sussex. It is resolved into sand-grains and then the whole process starts again and another cycle of millions of years begins once more.

III

KINDS OF PEBBLES

Their varieties of composition, texture, structure, colour and hardness. How to distinguish the commoner kinds of pebble one from another

We now come to the heart of the matter: the identification of pebbles. All who have read the previous chapters may have awaited this one with no little impatience. They may be still less patient on realizing that they must master a lesson in the rudiments of geology before they can begin to discern the nature and characteristics of the commoner sorts of pebble. But let them take heart. This lesson in 'geology with tears' will be brief.

Textbooks on the subject tend to be forbidding, as they are written in a scientific jargon comprised of long words derived from Greek, Latin and German. Doubtless, this terminology is essential to the professional geologist and the serious student of the subject, but it is baffling to the layman. In recent years some short and comparatively simple books for the general reader have appeared. The appended Book List mentions several of them.

There are three classes of rock: igneous, sedimentary and metamorphic. Every rock in the world must be one of the three.

1. IGNEOUS ROCKS, as their name (Latin: *ignis*, 'fire') suggests, are those which were formed under conditions of intense heat by the solidifying of molten material. This material has either been erupted by volcanic action out of the earth's crust and then has quickly cooled or been forced up towards the surface, beneath

which it has slowly cooled. Thus, we see that the igneous rocks are of two kinds: the volcanic, or extrusive, which are erupted in liquid form out of vents, such as the craters of volcanoes, and cool quickly; and the plutonic (so called after Pluto, the god of the underworld), or intrusive, which have been forced up, again in liquid form, towards, but not through, the earth's surface and in that position have cooled very slowly. Millions of years later, when that surface has been worn away by weather, the plutonic rocks are exposed.

Now let us glance briefly at each of these two kinds of igneous rock and select a few of their common varieties.

(a) *Volcanic*. We have no active volcanoes in Great Britain to-day, but this country was once the scene of widespread volcanic activity. Many of our mountains and hills are composed of hard rock, which was once hot molten matter that was erupted volcanically. Some of the mountains of North Wales and the Lake District are of volcanic origin, but we must not think of them as extinct volcanoes. They are the remnants of huge eruptions of lava and cinders ejected by volcanoes of which there is now no trace. The greatest spread of lava in the British Isles is in Antrim, in Northern Ireland. It covers 1,600 square miles, but even this is insignificant when compared with the vast lava flows in Asia and America. Those in the Deccan, in India, for instance, cover 200,000 square miles. The term 'flows' in this connection may be misleading. They were flows at one time and then only for a very short time, the period of rapid cooling. They have been solid and very hard for many millions of years.

Now, what are the main rocks that were formed in these volcanic flows? Leaving aside such eruptive products as volcanic ash (which, when compressed into a rock, is called 'tuff') and pumice, which, strangely enough, is a kind of glass, its sponge-like structure being due to the presence of steam and gas in the molten lava, we can select one rock as the main product of volcanic action. It is basalt.

Basalt is solidified lava. As the lava cooled too quickly for it to crystallize thoroughly, the tiny crystals in basalt cannot easily be detected without a microscope. It is dark, very hard and very compact. When rubbed down, it is very smooth to the touch. It has a habit, when cooling, of solidifying into hexagonal columns. Fingal's Cave, in the Isle of Staffa, provides a striking display of such columns. Another curious characteristic of basalt is its unwillingness to be ground down from a boulder to a pebble. Its hardness and compactness help it to withstand for a very long time the rubs and bumps of the tide and river, but it has a tendency to break up into fragments before it can be reduced to pebble size. There are basalt pebbles, of course, but they are few in proportion to the prevalence of the rock.

(b) *Plutonic*. Having cooled very slowly below ground, these rocks had ample time to crystallize naturally, so we have one certain means of distinguishing them from the volcanic rocks. We can call the plutonic rocks crystalline, and the volcanic rocks, so far as the naked eye is concerned, non-crystalline. Another distinguishing feature between the two kinds, also the result of the difference in their rates of cooling, is that the volcanic rocks are fine-grained and the plutonic rocks are coarse-grained. These contrasts in appearance and texture will be helpful to us when we come to examine pebbles more closely.

The most common and most familiar of all the plutonic rocks is granite. Great masses of it outcrop over considerable parts of the earth's surface, particularly among mountain ranges and on high ground which has been severely denuded by the weather of countless centuries. Dartmoor is one mass of it, extending for 200 square miles. It abounds in the Cornish peninsula, Cumberland, Westmorland, the Scottish Highlands, and the Mourne Mountains and Wicklow Hills in Ireland.

Let us look at a lump of Dartmoor or Cornish granite. With the naked eye we can see the three minerals of which it consists. One of them looks exactly like glass. This is quartz, one of the commonest minerals on earth. It consists of silica (oxide of silicon) and it constitutes about one-third of the lump. The large white crystals are those of another mineral, felspar (sometimes spelt 'feldspar'), also very common. It makes up the greater proportion of the rock. Thirdly, the little glistening black flakes are mica. There are several varieties of felspar and mica, so the names are those of groups or families of minerals and not of a specific variety. They vary very much in colour. The mica in common commercial use is white, yet in our piece of granite it is black. There is also a brown variety. Felspar in our specimen is a dull white. It can be pale pink and sometimes almost red. Then it imparts to the granite a slightly reddish hue. The rock's usual colour, however, is grey, like that of our Dartmoor specimen, because the dull white of the felspar, the colourlessness of the quartz and the black of the mica flakes combine to produce a general greyishness.

Of the other varieties of plutonic rock we can briefly consider two. They are much less abundant than granite, because they do not form such gigantic masses. They are dolerite and gabbro. Dolerite is a rock which has intruded itself when in a molten state between other rocks. When occupying a vertical space between those other rocks, the dolerite which filled it took the shape of a wall or, to give it its geological name, a dyke. When forcing its way between horizontal beds, the dolerite formed itself into a flat slab or, in geological language, a sill. So dolerite is usually found in either dykes or sills. As it cooled more rapidly than granite, its crystals are smaller, but they are easily discernible by the naked eye. The white ones are felspar. The other mineral in dolerite is augite, which gives the rock its dark colour, a deep brown that seems almost black. Sometimes the augite has a greenish tinge. The rock is both hard and heavy and is consequently in frequent use as road metal.

Gabbro. Unlike dolerite, this rock is not found in the form of dykes or sills but in large bosses or protruding lumps; but, like dolerite, it is very dark, very heavy and consists mainly of the same two minerals, felspar and augite. The difference in appearance and texture of the two rocks is simply this, that gabbro is much more coarsely grained than dolerite.

51

2. SEDIMENTARY ROCKS. This name is self-explanatory, for such a rock consists of sediments laid down in water, salt or fresh, and sometimes on dry land. The sediments have come from various sources. The main sources were: the breaking down of rocks exposed on the surface into small fragments by the action of sun, wind, rain and frost, the fragments being washed down into seas or lakes to form deposits; and the sinking down of organic remains into water.

In the former case the destruction of old rocks has led. to the formation of new rocks; in the latter case the death of innumerable creatures that lived in water has produced a deposit of the hard portions of their bodies and this deposit has ultimately consolidated into rock.

As some of the sedimentary rocks have come into existence as the result of the destruction of old rocks, it necessarily follows that some sedimentary rocks are derived from the breaking down of igneous rocks.

Sedimentary rocks make up the largest of the three classes of rock, because they cover the greater part of the earth's surface. Here, again, in order to distinguish between the processes by which the rocks came into existence, we must employ a subdivision into groups.

(a) *The Limestones*. The sediments that compose these very common rocks were laid down, grain by grain, in clear water. As the deposit thickened, so it was compressed by its own weight and hardened into rock, a process accelerated by a self-cementing quality possessed by all the little particles. Much of our limestone is formed from the skeletons or the fragments of skeletons of sea creatures: corals, sea-lilies (crinoids), sea-urchins, shells and so forth. All these skeletons contained carbonate of lime. If the limestone has undergone a high degree of crystallization we cannot detect the fossils of these little creatures in the stone, but when there has been little crystallization, the fossils can be detected by the thousand. Sometimes the rock consists entirely of the remains of one kind of creature. For example, some of the chalk, a very familiar kind of limestone, white, friable and rather soft, consists of minute sea organisms, called foraminifera, too small to be visible except through a microscope. Another limestone, called oolite, resembles the roe of a fish, being apparently comprised of millions of tiny eggs. These were originally sand grains, shell fragments or other tiny particles which received a coating of calcium carbonate from the water in which they were deposited and became compactly cemented together. Then there are limestones which consist entirely of the remains of corals, and others which are a mass of fossilized sea-lilies or crinoids. The latter is not uncommon and is called crinoidal limestone. Crinoids and large shells are sometimes found in chalk.

The massive limestone of our hilly districts is the hard, crystalline kind. Great, irregular blocks of it are quarried for building purposes. Hard though it looks, however, it dissolves, as all other limestones do, in weak acid and can be penetrated to great depths by water which has become slightly acid through the absorption of carbon dioxide from the air. Consequently, it is in the regions abounding in limestone that we are most likely to come upon caverns and gorges. Of all the common rocks limestone is the only one that can be easily eroded by very weak acid.

(b) *The Sandstones and Grits.* We paid some attention to sandstone in the last chapter, but we must examine it more closely. Its name is simple and accurate, because the rock consists wholly of sand-grains. These grains could have been deposited in the sea, in fresh water or on dry land. If on land they must have been laid down when this country was undergoing desert conditions. There are very massive formations of sandstone in Britain which were deposited under those conditions. It is called the New Red Sandstone. The term 'new' may seem to be a misnomer when applied to rocks which came into existence at least 190,000,000 years ago, but it is used in comparison with the Old Red Sandstone, which is some 90,000,000 years older still. The latter may also have been laid down on dry land or, possibly, in shallow water. It is important to remember that these two sandstones are not the only ones.

There were other deposits in the long course of geological time, some of which are yellowish, some brownish and some greyish.

The nature of the grains is a guide to the manner in which the rock was formed. Desert sand-grains are very small and well-rounded. Sand-grains laid down in the sea are a little angular, while the grains in river sands are more angular. Nearly all the grains consist of quartz, but other minerals, sometimes a host of them, reveal themselves in very small proportions on analysis of the sandstone. The stone varies greatly in its hardness, its colour and the size and angularity of its grains, and it is not easy to decide precisely at what point a hard and tightly compressed sandstone becomes a grit. Obviously, a stone formed of well-rounded, almost spherical grains is more porous and therefore more easily crumbled than one formed of angular, flattish grains. The former is certainly a sandstone and the latter a grit, but the dividing line is blurred. Moreover, there is a sandstone of great hardness and toughness, consisting almost entirely of quartz grains closely held together by a silica cement. This is called quartzite. It is a fascinating rock and will repay closer study when we come to examine the pebbles that are made of it.

Grits are coarse-grained sandstones, the grains being more angular. The best known is Millstone Grit, so called because it provided excellent material for millstones and grindstones. There are huge deposits of the rock, some of which are thousands of feet thick, in Derbyshire and the Pennines.

There is a fairly common rock which is neither sandstone nor grit, but is more appropriately classified with them than in any other category of sedimentary rocks. It is Conglomerate, or pudding-stone. Instead of sand-grains it consists of pebbles held together by some cementing material. The pebbles themselves may be compounded of fragments of rock of many kinds. Conglomerate rocks are usually the surviving parts of ancient beaches, but the deposits which form them could have been laid down in the sea or on river-beds.

(c) *Shales and Slates*. The original material of these rocks was clay, great beds of which were laid down in the shallow waters where rivers join the sea. Shale is clay, consolidated and compressed. It is a laminated rock, made up of very thin layers, each of which marks a stage in the thickening of the original clay bed. The pressures it underwent have helped to make it fissile—that is, to split into these thin layers when a sharp instrument is forced in between any two of them. There are very extensive and very thick deposits of the rock in Britain and some of them form part of our cliff scenery, notably at Whitby, on the Yorkshire coast. The rock is dark grey, very fine-grained and of smooth texture, as one would expect a consolidated clay to be.

Shale is often present in beds of great thickness in coal-mining districts, the coal-seams running through the beds. This shale contains the remnants of plants, pressed and fossilized, which grew in the age when coal was being formed from vegetable deposits.

Slate was originally shale or clay. It has suffered terrific pressure from movements of the earth's crust in those remote ages when the surface buckled and mountain-chains were raised. So the natural setting of slate is in mountainous or very hilly districts. The great pressures it has endured have crushed out of existence the laminations or bedding layers that marked its growth as a shale and have substituted cleavage layers at an angle that bears no relation to the bedding. These cleavage planes appear to be at right angles to the direction in which the pressure came. The slates cleave easily along these planes into very thin slices. This property, together with their durability and imperviousness to water, gives them their great value as roofing material. Slate is more lustrous than shale, because the greater pressure that it has undergone has made it slightly crystalline. Very minute flakes of mica and other minerals give slate its sheen. The rock has a slightly purple tinge, but there are variations in colour from greyish-green to reddish-purple.

We must not leave the sedimentary rocks without reference to two very common rocks from which multitudes of pebbles are formed but which are not sedimentary in the strictest sense of having been deposited as sediments. We can class them with this group because they always form part of sedimentary formations. They are flint and chert.

Flint, like quartz, is solid silica; but quartz is crystalline, and flint is non-crystalline; and it is easy to distinguish one from the other. The usual setting of flint is inside a mass of chalk, either in the form of continuous bands or layers or of nodules or lumps. If we look up from the beach to a white cliff of chalk we see the thousands of dark flints in strong contrast with the whiteness of the chalk in which they are embedded. How did the intruders get there? Geologists are not completely sure, but the generally accepted view is that the flints were not deposited while the chalk was being laid down. The silica which is slightly soluble in water flowed into the joints and bedding-planes of the chalk at a later stage and then solidified. Much of it entered into the spaces occupied by fossil sponges and sea-urchins. They abounded in the chalk sea and their skeletons were deposited by the million in the chalk bed. The liquid silica absorbed the skeletons completely and their outlines can still be traced very clearly in the flint nodules.

Sometimes we find flint in beds of brown clay some little distance from chalk. The clay is the product left after the more soluble parts of the chalk have been dissolved in water. The water has washed out this residue, carrying away the insoluble flints with it. The result is a bed of material known as clay-with-flints. Where we find such a bed we can assume that near to it there was once a thick bed of chalk.

The influence of flint upon the history of early man was very great. As soon as he had discovered that a broken flint has a sharp edge of considerable hardness and keenness, he began to fashion flint implements of many kinds and went on doing so for untold thousands of years. This was one of the reasons why there were large settlements of people in our chalk-lands for many years after the dawning of the Bronze Age.

Chert differs only slightly from flint. It originated in much the same manner, usually occurring in limestone in the same way as flint occurs in chalk. In many of the cherts found in limestone, the silica of the chert has replaced the calcium carbonate of the limestone, but traces of the original structure of the limestone are still preserved. Chert is usually grey, brown or black in colour, flint varies from dark grey, through brown, to nearly black.

3. METAMORPHIC ROCKS. Once more the name indicates the nature of the rock. Metamorphosis means change of form (Greek: *meta*, 'change'; *morphe*, 'form'), but there is more than change of form in these rocks. There is often a considerable change of character. Originally, they were all very old rocks and every one of them must have been either igneous or sedimentary before the change. Great heat or great pressure, or both, were the causes of the change. If that is so, you might well ask, why is not slate a metamorphic rock? Well, to some extent it has experienced change, but not so much as to alter its form and nature out of recognition. It still possesses some of the characteristics of a sedimentary rock.

There are various kinds of metamorphism, but we can confine our attention to the two main ones: local and regional.

Local metamorphism comes about when a mass of plutonic material pushes its way up among other rocks and slowly cools, giving off, in that process, heat of hundreds of degrees centigrade. The effect upon the surrounding rocks is severe. They melt, absorb new minerals from the plutonic intruder and then re-crystallize. As heat rather than pressure is the agent in such cases, the change can also be called thermal metamorphism.

Regional metamorphism is far more important for the simple reason that its effect is not merely local but widespread, sometimes covering thousands of square miles. A combination of heat and pressure produces it. Imagine the creation of a huge mass of sedimentary rock at the time when this country lay beneath the sea. The depositing of sediments through millions of years, and to a depth of hundreds of feet, buries the older rocks and exerts upon them an enormous pressure. This in turn produces great heat and a disturbance of the earth's surface in that region. The buried rocks are crushed, sheared and melted. Millions of years elapse, the land rises and the thick sedimentary cover wears away under the very gradual denuding action of sun, wind, frost and rain. The original surface rocks are exposed again, but they are unrecognizable. In solidifying they have changed their mineral content and have re-crystallized; and, under the crushing weight of the mass that lay above them, they have suffered a change of form. The convulsive earth movements have also had a shattering effect. Such is regional metamorphism, also termed dynamic metamorphism because movement and pressure, as well as heat, have produced it. Almost the whole of the northern half of Scotland consists of metamorphic rocks. They are fairly extensive in Anglesey, but in England the outcrops are few and small. Cornwall, Devon, Cumberland, Westmorland and the Malvern Hills contain some well-known examples.

The three most familiar of the metamorphic rocks are gneiss, schist and marble.

Gneiss (pronounced 'nice') is a word of German origin, derived from an Old High German verb *gneistan*, 'to sparkle'. In sunshine, especially after rain, it certainly does sparkle, as it is a highly crystalline rock. Its outstanding characteristic is that it is banded or streaked. Gneiss is usually metamorphosed granite and, if not granite, a plutonic rock of similar composition. But, whereas in granite the mineral crystals of quartz, felspar and mica are intermingled, in gneiss they are arranged in bands or streaks. Such an arrangement is called foliation. The coarse-grained layers or foliae of crystals give the rock a very attractive appearance.

Schist (pronounced 'shist') is derived from a Greek word *schistos*, meaning 'easily split'. This is an accurate description. Like slate, it has innumerable planes of cleavage and very thin layers can be split away from it. Its foliations are much narrower than those of gneiss and it is also more finely grained. The shimmering lustre of schist in the sunlight is fascinating. Mica and quartz are the two minerals of which the rock is usually composed. Their glittering qualities impart the sheen to it. Another property possessed by schist that helps us to distinguish it from gneiss and other metamorphic rocks is its flakiness.

Marble is metamorphosed limestone. The carbonate of lime (or calcium carbonate) of which limestone is mainly composed is re-crystallized into a granular mosaic of a very pleasing texture and appearance. It can have any one of a large range of colours and is consequently in great demand for the ornate pillars and interior decoration of spacious and impressive buildings.

Now, although we have affirmed that every rock must belong to one of the three classes—igneous, sedimentary and metamor-phic—we must realize that the boundaries separating the groups are not sharply defined. Slate, for instance, a partly metamor-phosed clay or shale, comes under the heading of sedimentary. We have also included quartzite in that class, because the change in the structure of many quartzite rocks from the original sand-stone has been only partial, but there are quartzites which display an almost total change. The re-crystallizing of the quartz grains and their close interlocking has made the rock more compact and more lustrous. The grains show no traces of their sedimentary origin. Thus it is possible for a partly metamorphosed quartzite to be classed as sedimentary and one that is almost completely changed as metamorphic. This classification is not made to be-wilder the student by creating exceptions to the rule. It is, after all, just common sense to allot a rock to the class to which it is most applicable.

This ends the lesson in geology. It is most desirable, indeed essential, to keep it in mind, for we depend upon it to aid us in the task of recognizing the pebbles on the beach. As an aid to memory here is a very compressed summary of the lesson in the form of a family tree:

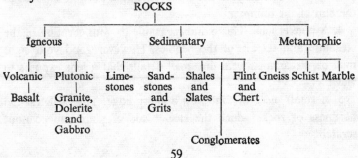

And now to the beach, to pick up the pebbles that attract our eye, to determine their origin and to decide what kind of journeys they have made.

First of all, is any special equipment necessary? Yes, if you intend to be a serious and earnest beachcomber (in the better sense of that usually opprobrious term). You will find the following of great service:

1. A geological map of the district (see the Book List in the Appendix). This will show you the geology of the whole region behind the coast. You will then know at once the nature of the cliffs or soil above the beach. This is knowledge of the utmost value, for, as you have already seen, the local rock is one of the major contributory sources of the beach pebbles.

2. A knife that has at least one strong blade. You will have frequent recourse to this for the scraping and scratching of the pebbles: scraping, in order to remove part of the skin they have acquired in their wanderings, and scratching, to test the hardness of the stone—a very necessary aid to the detection of its nature.

3. A small hammer with a fairly heavy head. Scraping with the knife does not always reveal the surface of the pebble clearly. The only way to see the texture and structure of the pebble in all its clarity is to make a fresh fracture—that is, to break off a piece of it. If you crash one stone against another you risk the loss of an eye. That would not only bring your seaside holiday abruptly to an end but rob you of your zest for pebble-hunting once and for all. The easiest and safest way to break a corner off a pebble is to place your foot firmly on the stone, leaving a portion exposed to the aim of the hammer.

4. A pocket lens. This is indispensable to your scrutiny of the structure and texture of the pebbles. However good your sight may be, it cannot reveal the small details that a lens exposes to view.

5. A small piece of flint with a sharp edge. This will test the hardness of rocks which the steel blade of your knife cannot scratch.

It may well be, however, that you prefer to conduct your pebble quest from the depths of a deck-chair, making an occasional effort to stretch out a hand towards a pebble that attracts you. Even in this posture of luxurious sloth you can enjoy the hunt, but you cannot pursue your inquiries to a satisfactory conclusion unless you take home your selection of pebbles and then subject them to knife, hammer and lens. The nature of some of them may be obvious at a glance—for instance, flint and quartzite. Of those not so obvious, be sure to take home a pair of each, because you may have to maltreat one of the pair with knife and hammer.

Here we must sound a note of warning and possibly of discouragement. Although the reading of this book, aided by your own patience, persistence and zeal, should enable you in time to identify most of the pebbles that were originally fragments of the commoner rocks, you will find many that baffle you. But this need not dishearten you, for some of them also baffle the professional geologist, equipped though he may be with a sound knowledge of crystallography, petrology and mineralogy. In order to ascertain with precision the contents of a pebble of peculiar structure, he has to take it to his laboratory, cut off an extremely thin slice of it with a rock-slicing apparatus and examine the slice through a petrological microscope fitted with polarizing and analysing prisms, a rotating stage and other refinements. He can thus determine, in their correct proportions, the minerals of which the pebble consists, their mutual relations and the order of their crystallization.

But all this is beyond our ken. We must be content to plod along the beach and to get all the help we can from our more homely appliances.

Let us imagine ourselves on any pebble beach on the coastline of England and Wales. Having studied the geological map of the district, we have already made a good start in the search, because we know what the local rocks are and that they will be well represented among the pebbles. We have also noted whether there are any rivers in the neighbourhood and, if so, what rocks they flow through. The shingle will contain a fair contribution from those rocks also. Finally, remembering from Chapter II the little summary of the prevalent drift directions along the coast, we know whether the shingle tends to move along the beach from left to right or from right to left. This will tell us from what parts of the coast most of the remaining pebbles have come. Our geological map must now be consulted again to give us some notion of the nature of the rocks that form those other parts of the coast. So, before beginning the search, we have a very rough idea of what we are likely to find.

The uninitiated pebble-seeker, perhaps attracted by the fresh, clean look of the belt of shingle from which the tide has recently receded, feels tempted to confine his search to that strip of the beach. This is not often the happiest of hunting-grounds. The upper belts of shingle that lie below high-water mark have also been washed by the sea not many hours before and will probably yield a richer store. This is especially true of beaches of the lonelier kind.

On picking up a pebble, particularly a well-travelled one, and asking yourself which of the three classes of rock it belongs to, you may be at a total loss, because it is completely covered by the skin or coating it has acquired on its journeys. The skin is often a thin crust of carbonate of lime. It obscures the true surface entirely and you may at once leap to the conclusion that you are holding a pebble of chalk or of whitish limestone. The old adage about appearances being deceitful applies with especial force to pebbles. That is why a strong knife is an essential item in your equipment. With it you can lay bare part of the surface of the pebble. You may even find that the pebble has grown two coats of differing colours. Scrape hard until you have scoured these integuments away from a square inch or so of the surface. Then you may begin to find an answer to your question.

The colour of the outer skin can be very deceptive to people who are reluctant to make thorough investigation. Long exposure to the weather has bleached many pebbles a dirty white or grey.

Some that have lain for long in pools that contained iron in solution have a thin reddish coating of oxide of iron, others may have a greenish tinge given them by carbonate of copper, or a staining of black by oxide of manganese.

What has your scraping revealed? Of one thing we can be certain. The pebble will show truly the original bedding and structure of the rock of which it once formed a part. Your first task is to decide whether it was igneous, sedimentary or metamorphic. Of the three, the one that reveals its nature most clearly is the sedimentary, simply because you can see the sediments themselves: the round grains of the sandstone, the more angular grains of the grit, the comparatively soft and powdery white grains of chalk and its minute marine organisms, the pudding-like make-up of the conglomerate, the fish-roe appearance of oolitic limestone, the fossilized remains in the crinoidal, coral or other fossiliferous limestone or the very compact and slightly crystalline grains of the massive limestone that bears no fossils. Here, again, the knife will help to narrow down the search, as it will easily scratch chalk and any kind of limestone.

A pebble of flint, once you have exposed part of its original surface to view, is self-revealing, despite its lack of sediments, by its hardness, the very sharp edge of any fragment you break away from it, its horny look and its habit of appearing to be translucent or not entirely opaque. If the pebble looks and feels like flint, but is much lighter in colour, you have good reason to think it is chert, yet some chert is almost black.

Slate should also make itself known to you by its slightly purple colour and by its readiness to split when you press the knife-blade down among its cleavage-planes. A pebble of shale, however, is less easily recognizable. It is helpful to remember that shale is consolidated clay and looks just what you would expect such clay to look like. It is also less compact than slate and, on being scraped by the knife, powders rather easily. Breathe on it and you may detect a slightly earthy smell.

Now, let us suppose that after a very careful scrutiny you have

① Ovoid pebble of grey granite

② Grey granite, with one surface cut and polished

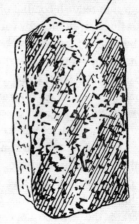

③ Pebble of schist, with one surface cut and polished. The laminations are more clearly seen on the uncut surface

④ Flattened ovoid pebble of crystalline limestone [unpolished]

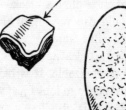

⑤ Fragment of whitish chert. Its angularities show that it has not been smoothed by the action of the tides for long

⑥ Portion of a rounded flint pebble. Note the thick white coating that the grey flint has acquired on the beach

⑦ Well-rounded pebble of fine-grained red sandstone

⑧ Flattened ovoid pebble of conglomerate

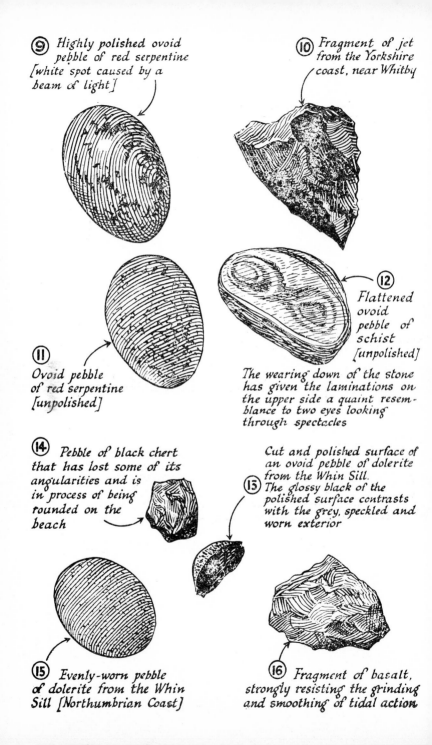

9 Highly polished ovoid pebble of red serpentine [white spot caused by a beam of light]

10 Fragment of jet from the Yorkshire coast, near Whitby

12 Flattened ovoid pebble of schist [unpolished]

The wearing down of the stone has given the laminations on the upper side a quaint resemblance to two eyes looking through spectacles

11 Ovoid pebble of red serpentine [unpolished]

14 Pebble of black chert that has lost some of its angularities and is in process of being rounded on the beach

13 Cut and polished surface of an ovoid pebble of dolerite from the Whin Sill. The glossy black of the polished surface contrasts with the grey, speckled and worn exterior

15 Evenly-worn pebble of dolerite from the Whin Sill [Northumbrian Coast]

16 Fragment of basalt, strongly resisting the grinding and smoothing of tidal action

(17) *Piece of amber from the coast of Suffolk*

(19) *Broken piece of chalcedony*

(18) *Carnelian pebble, highly polished*

(20) *Oval slice polished and commercial* *of onyx stained for purposes*

(21) *Amber pebble, highly polished*

(23) *Ovoid pebble of Carnelian, unpolished*

(22) *Pebble of onyx. The banding is faintly discernible through the beach coating*

(26) *Pebble of citrine, with whitish beach coating*

(25) *Oval slice of agate pebble, polished and stained for commercial purposes*

(27) *Citrine pebble, highly polished*

(24) *Pebble of "fortification" agate. The ground plan of the "fortress" can be seen on the polished side*

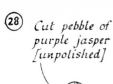
28 Cut pebble of purple jasper [unpolished]

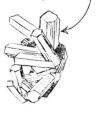
29 Group of quartz prisms

30 Flattened cylindrical pebble of green serpentine

31 Well-rounded pebble of opaque quartz

32 Fragment of gabbro with one side cut and polished

33 Ovoid pebble of grit, veined with quartz

34 Polished pebble of purple jasper

35 Ovoid pebble of quartzite with broken side uppermost, revealing the structure of tightly compacted grains

36 Ovoid pebble of slate, with a quartz vein running through it

decided that the pebble is not of sedimentary rock. Then it must be igneous or metamorphic. Well, if it is metamorphic, it will have one of the following qualities: the banding of gneisses, the finer foliations and flakiness of the schists, the compact and glittering crystallization of the quartzites or the crystal mosaic of marble. Only large pebbles, naturally, can display the broad banding of the gneisses.

Let us now assume that the pebble possesses none of these characteristics. Then you are forced to the conclusion that it is formed of igneous rock. Which of them? Take first the plutonic rocks, which occupy a much larger area of this country than the volcanic. The qualities that distinguish them are their very marked degree of crystallization resulting from the medley of minerals that compose them, their lack of foliation and lamination and their pronounced hardness, toughness and weight. Enough has been said already of the texture and structure of the more familiar ones: granite, dolerite and gabbro, to guide you some little way towards their identification. If the pebble is of granite and you have made a fresh fracture in it, you will not need the pocket lens to see the three minerals that compose it. Nor will you need it to differentiate the coarse-grained gabbro from the finer-grained dolerite. In both of them the white or greyish crystals of felspar are visible to the naked eye.

Our one representative of the volcanic rocks, the solidified lava, basalt, is more difficult to identify. Its hardness, heaviness, smoothness, very fine-grained nature and iron-black colouring should help you to distinguish it from all other members of the igneous family.

By a process of exhaustion, such as the one above, you can narrow down the field of inquiry to a small group of rocks and, with widening experience and extending study, often to one rock. But it cannot be emphasized too strongly that the procedure outlined above is a simplification, probably an over-simplification, of the lines of inquiry to be followed in the attempt to identify the rock of which a pebble is made. In order to avoid complexity of treatment we have selected only a few of the common rocks as examples. Not only are there many others, but there are other varieties of those we have mentioned. Still, that need not daunt you, for once your interest in, and curiosity about, pebbles have been aroused you will take pleasure in the reading of books on geology that are not too highly technical. Your surest aid to familiarity with rocks is to make regular visits to a geological museum. London readers will find all, and more than all, they want in the Geological Museum and in the Natural History Museum (Department of Mineralogy), both of which are in South Kensington.

After that little digression we can return to our beach. There are one or two other properties possessed by certain pebbles which can help us towards correct classification. One of them is their shape. We have already referred to this in the first chapter, where you read that there are three usual shapes: spheres, ovoids and flattened ovoids (or discs); and one less usual: cylinders with rounded ends. Roughly—indeed, very roughly—speaking, the igneous rocks tend to become spherical pebbles, as they have the same hard crystalline structure throughout and become evenly rubbed down or worn away. If not spherical they develop an ovoid form resembling that of a broad egg, the longer diameter not greatly exceeding the shorter. Of the sedimentary rocks, flint resists the rubbing and bumping on the beach for a very long time, so a flint pebble is more likely than other stones to display a few corners that have yet to be rubbed off. In time, of course, all nodules of flint lose their angularity and generally become thick ovoids. The very hard, compact sandstone and quartzites, like the igneous rocks, withstand wear fairly equally from all directions and take for the most part a shape between the spherical and the ovoid. The harder limestones are mostly ovoid and the softer ones, together with the softer sandstones and the shales and slates, flattened ovoids. There is much variation in the shape of the metamorphic rocks. In spite of the foliated nature of the gneisses, their great hardness and their crystalline structure help them to resist erosion and so their shape is usually between spherical and ovoid, but the finer laminations of schist and its extreme flakiness make it less resistant. Schist pebbles therefore vary in shape between ovoid and flattened ovoid. Marble, which is crystalline throughout and is neither foliated nor flaky, strenuously resists the rubbing down on the beach and so tends to become a more spherical than ovoid pebble. We have already noted that when a fragment, much longer than it is broad, is torn from a rock it tends to take the form of a narrow cylinder. The majority of pebbles of this rather unusual shape are schist.

We occasionally find pebbles that are piriform (pear-shaped). The material that once surrounded the narrow end must, evidently, have been softer than the rest of the pebble. On the south coast of Devonshire there is an extraordinary lagoon, Slapton Ley, nearly two miles long, cut off from the sea by a bar of shingle. Here are to be found among the flints many small piriform pebbles of white quartz.

There are pebbles which disclose their identity to you when you feel them, provided always that you are feeling their true surface. The best-known example of them is serpentine, so called because its colouring suggests the appearance of a snake-skin. Serpentine is an igneous (plutonic) rock which has been partly metamorphosed by contact with water. The mineral, olivine, of which it was mainly composed in its original state, has been changed and softened to serpentine. It is a highly attractive rock, usually of a very pleasing green. The most prominent mass of it in Britain is the Lizard headland, in Cornwall. It forms nearly all the headland. Much of the Lizard serpentine is green, but some of it is a dark red. Serpentine pebbles are usually ovoids and they possess a wax-like lustre. To touch them after the removal of their coating is to become aware of a sensation that can best be described as caressing, but some unimaginative people have been content to call it soapy. That adjective is best applied to another rock called steatite, popularly known as soapstone. It is a compact variety of talc, the softest of all minerals, easily scratched by the finger-nail.

Some pebbles have been called firestones because they produce sparks when struck, or violently rubbed, together. Everybody knows that flint behaves in this way, but not so many people are aware that pebbles of quartz and of metamorphic quartzite, when so treated, produce bigger and better sparks. Take two quartzite pebbles, or break one of them into two pieces, and strike one against the other in darkness. An orange-coloured flash results. There is also a smell, not unpleasant, but very difficult to describe. It is still more difficult to account for the fact that, if you strike the stones together under water, they will then emit an exactly similar flash and smell. So, if you are doubtful whether a pebble consists of quartzite or not, you have only to conduct this simple experiment.

If your beach lies north of the line marking the farthest advance of the ice-sheets, the limits of which were described in Chapter II, you may find among the pebbles some of the long-distance travellers, including even some formed from the rocks of Scandinavia. But you must not assume that beaches south of the line will be entirely free from such pebbles. A river, as we have already noted, could have carried them over the last stage of the journey. They could also have arrived on a southern beach as passengers on, or in, a floating block of ice. The melting of the sheets at the end of the Ice Age must have dislodged portions of them from the main body and these blocks or bergs, floating into slightly warmer waters, must have released, as they melted, the pebbles embedded in them.

Of course, if your beach is bounded by land containing layers of boulder-clay, you can expect to find a bountiful assortment of ice-borne pebbles gathered from the rocks of regions near and far. Such a beach is always interesting, as its contents are usually very varied and they present the pebble-hunter with more than enough problems to hold his interest.

Pebbles that have been ice-borne during any part of their journey from the parent rock to the beach on which you find them can disclose that fact to you by their appearance, but they can do so only if the glacier scraped them against other rocks, either in the act of scooping them up or in carrying them along beneath it, frozen into its underside. Then the glacial pebbles may bear unmistakable marks of their rough journey. If so, they will be grooved, scratched or faceted—that is, one part of the pebble will appear to have been planed down flat. The grooves in a glacial pebble, as we have already seen, are called striations. If you cannot see them on the surface of a pebble, you must not assume that it is not glacial. It could have been scooped up with a mass of other small rocks by the glacier, thus completing its journey unmarked. On the other hand, many pebbles that were formerly striated have been worn down and have lost their striations.

To many pebble-seekers the striated glacial pebble, bearing the marks that tell of its long and hazardous journey, is the most fascinating of all, but to others, who look for colour, glitter and lustre in their pebbles, it neither arouses their interest nor evokes their imagination. They search for the gleaming quartzite, the crystalline gneiss, the lustrous, apple-green schist, the bright red, yellow or green jasper, the conglomerate with its medley of patterns and colours, the marble with its crystal mosaic, or the waxlike serpentine. Perhaps they are attracted most of all by the pebbles of porphyritic texture. This is to be seen fairly often in many pebbles of igneous origin, e.g. granite. The crystals of felspar and quartz, instead of having their usual appearance of being closely intermingled, are conspicuously visible, because they are surrounded and outlined by fine-grained material. Against this darker background they seem to stand out in crystalline beauty. A porphyritic pebble, cut and polished, is a delight to the eye. The word 'porphyry' comes from the Greek and means 'like purple'. The Greeks and Romans imported from a quarry in Egypt a porphyritic stone of purple hue and used it for decorative purposes in their buildings. There is no purple tinge in any of our porphyritic rocks, as the word has lost much of its original meaning.

Other pebble enthusiasts find joy in the quest for fossil-bearing pebbles. Their texture, when cut and polished, is also delightful.

As there are fossils innumerable, we could occupy much of this book in describing them, but we must limit ourselves to a few of the common ones. Readers who wish to study fossils in detail should consult one of the many textbooks on palaeontology.

Fossils are the remains of animals or plants preserved in rocks. The study of them is a highly important branch of geology, because they tell the story of the history of much of the earth's surface and of the creatures that lived on it through the ages. The first man to discover that each stratum, or layer, of rock is characterized by the organic remains it contains was the great William Smith (1769–1839), justly called 'the father of English Geology'. From this beginning he was able to build up a table of the comparative ages of the strata and thus enabled geologists to compile a life-history of the earth. This history is still incomplete, for, though there are millions of fossils in the rocks, they portray only a fraction of all the life that was going on at the time when the rocks they now occupy were being laid down. Smith had next to no education and wrote very little, but in 1815 he published the first geological map of England and Wales. It embodied the results of all his researches. As the work of a man who was the product of a village school it was a rare achievement.

Almost all fossils occupy sedimentary rocks. Why? They would have been crushed to fragments by the pressure exerted upon metamorphic rocks, by the violent convulsions of the earth's surface, and their skeletons would never have survived the high temperatures that accompanied those movements. The igneous rocks of the plutonic kind pushed their way up from below the crust where no life went on at all; those of the volcanic kind were erupted from the boiling mass below, where life was impossible. Yet it is possible for rocks formed of volcanic ash to contain a few fossils. Obviously, the organisms must have entered the volcanic ash after it had cooled and before it was compressed into a rock.

The sedimentary rocks which are richest in fossils are limestone, chalk and shale. This is not surprising, as all of them were slowly deposited under water, and these are ideal conditions for the preservation of organic remains. The vast majority of the fossils in these rocks are consequently those of marine creatures. In the chalk, which was laid down in clear water, we must expect to find the remnants of organisms which inhabited such water, but in the shale, which is consolidated clay, we look for the fossils of those creatures whose habitat was muddy water.

With a hammer and a small chisel we can easily extract the fossils from a cliff of soft limestone or shale, while from a cliff of chalk we can remove them with a knife-blade. Flint will not yield its fossils at all.

Although we have defined fossils as the remains of animals or plants preserved in rocks, we must not be misled into thinking that every fossil is a remnant of an actual animal or plant. It is very often the cast image or mould of the organism. Long after the creature, bone or leaf became entombed in the hardening rock, it may have decayed and finally left in the rock an exact mould of itself. Silica, carbonate of lime, or other material which is carried in solution, then gradually filled up the space and formed a hard replica of the departed organism. For example, a shell-fish dies and is washed into a slowly forming bed of sediment. The creature itself disappears in time and the space it occupied is filled with mineral matter brought by water through the porous rock. That matter solidifies and forms a perfect mould of the shell-fish. The shell, however, is preserved and may still be there when you dig the fossil out. But if the shell has also decayed, or has not been replaced by sediment, the little ridges and cavities will be those of the *inside* of the shell, giving you the impression that the creature had worn its shell inside out. If the original shell is still in existence or has been replaced when you find the fossil, its markings will be, of course, the natural ones, those on the outside of the shell.

Very often the teeth and bone of a fossilized creature and the harder seeds and roots of the fossilized plant have been preserved intact in the encasing rock, their hardness having saved them from disintegration. The minerals that have replaced the softer parts

71

make so close a copy of them that it is not always easy to distinguish those parts of the fossil which have been preserved and those which have been replaced by a mineral mould. Even the slightest traces of the past life of a creature or plant rank as fossils for geologists regard as fossils the impressions of organisms. Thus the tracks and burrowings of worms and the footprints of birds, reptiles and mammals all rank as fossils. So also do the droppings of reptiles and fishes. These droppings are called coprolites (Greek: *Kopros*, 'dung'). They have provided the most valuable evidence to geologists of the creatures that existed during the ages when the strata that now enclose them were in process of formation.

And now let us glance at some of the more familiar fossils.

Graptolites (Greek: graptos = engraved or painted; lithos = stone), long ago extinct, were little marine creatures of low organization. Thin horny rods, some of which resemble tuning-forks in shape, supported them, each individual creature occupying one small cup-like cavity. The cavities were linked together by a common canal or channel of living matter. The fossilized remains of the rods look like fretsaw blades, the teeth having been formed by one side of the outer edge of each cavity. The fossils abound in the darker shales and slates. Many of the rods are single, some are double and have a forked shape, and others have several branches.

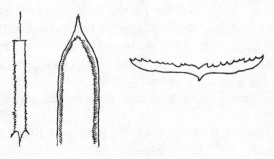

FIGURE 4

Trilobites, meaning creatures with a three-lobed body, have also been extinct for hundreds of millions of years, though they lasted longer than the graptolites and were of a much higher organization. They were the earliest of the crustacea, the group of creatures represented to-day by lobsters, crabs, crayfish, prawns and shrimps. The three lobes can be seen in the simplified drawing below, which shows the fossil as it is usually found in the limestone and the shales. They vary very much in size and in structure. Their appearance is slightly suggestive of a large woodlouse.

FIGURE 5

Brachiopods (Greek: brachion = an arm; pous, podos = a foot) were shell-fish. Their popular name is lamp-shells, as some of them resemble the oil-lamp of ancient Rome. As the soft body is contained within a double, hinged shell, the brachiopod is a member of that large class of shell-fish called bivalves. Each of the two valves (or shells) is symmetrical about a line drawn through its centre. In this respect it differs from several other

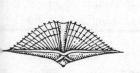 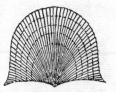 

FIGURE 6

bivalves. The shell of the brachiopod varies so much in its shape and pattern that a picture of a typical brachiopod is not easy to draw. Three of the common varieties are shown above. Sometimes the shell is thin and glassy, at other times it is more solid and less lustrous, but in nearly all instances it is very attractive. Limestones and shales contain vast numbers of the fossil. Note in the three drawings the concentric lines running roughly parallel to the outer edge of the shell. A similar ornamentation is to be seen on the shells of certain other bivalves, such as cockles.

Crinoids, or sea-lilies. Both the name and the appearance of these fossils are misleading. They suggest a plant, but the crinoid was an animal. A long flexible stem attached it to the sea-floor. Almost all its fossilized remains are fragments of the stem, which was much harder than the calyx at its top end. The calyx was almost the whole of the animal. The crinoid of later ages had no stem, but, like its predecessor, had arms that closely resembled the stem. Millions of these fragmental stems and arms occupy limestone cliffs and headlands. Indeed, there are some massive limestone formations that consist almost wholly of them; the stone is consequently called crinoidal limestone.

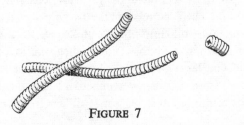

FIGURE 7

Ammonites, so called because the creature lived in a spirally-curved shell resembling the ram's horn on the statue of Jupiter Ammon. The fossil is popularly known as a snake-stone, because its spirals suggest a coiled-up snake. It has some thousands of varieties and is one of the commonest of fossils abounding in limestone and shale. The fossils can be seen to great advantage in the East Cliff at Whitby, on the Yorkshire coast. Probably

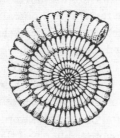

FIGURE 8

the name of snake-stone originated from a Whitby legend, to
which Sir Walter Scott refers in his poem, 'Marmion':

> *Thus the nuns of Whitby told,*
> *How of thousand snakes, each one*
> *Was changed into a coil of stone,*
> *When holy Hilda prayed:*
> *Themselves within their sacred bound*
> *Their stony folds had often found.*

We have wandered some distance from the subject of pebbles,
but the excursion has not been purposeless. Many long stretches
of our coast are backed by cliffs of limestone, chalk, shale and
sandstone; and the pebbles in the beaches below those cliffs are
rich in fossils. It is, therefore, most desirable that you should be
able to recognize the common ones. In so doing you will assuredly
feel an urge to make a wider and deeper study of fossils. Moreover,
the zealous pebble-collector is always eager to have the choicest
of his finds cut and polished so that the delicate tracery of the
intermingled crystals, the porphyritic structure, the marble mosaic
or the outline and detail of the embedded fossil stand out in
fascinating clarity. And his interest is all the keener if he is not
only able to name the rock of which the pebble consists but also
to identify the kind of fossil it contains.

To the casual beholder a lump of flint may appear to be
nothing more than a piece of hard, homogeneous silica, but to

the eye of one who knows how the flint nodules came to be inside the bed of chalk it can reveal much more. He looks for, and very often finds, in the flint traces of the skeleton of the organism around which the liquid silica solidified. Very frequently this is a fossil sponge, which betrays its presence in a complicated and very pleasing pattern of little spikes. These needle-like rods are the petrified remains of the framework of the sponge. They are called spicula (the plural of the Latin word: spiculum = a small sharp point). They do not readily reveal themselves to the naked eye, because the surface of the translucent flint has been bleached and coated. Break off a flake of the flint, hold it up to the light and you will then know whether the pebble is worthy of further scrutiny. In all likelihood you will see some small, opaque spots in the horny, translucent flint, perhaps a minute fragment of a shell or the impression of a shell, possibly some tiny corals or the scales of primitive fish. If you see any spicula you have good reason to think that the pebble contains some part, at least, of a fossil sponge. The spicula display themselves to the best advantage if the pebble is broken in half and one of the two interior surfaces is cut and polished by a lapidary. Then the colour, delicacy and complexity of the spicula make up a most pleasing intaglio.

When Brighton became a fashionable resort in Regency days a craze for pebble-collecting and polishing began and it continued well into the reign of Queen Victoria. Lapidaries were busy, cutting and polishing flint pebbles that contained fossil sponges and other marine organisms. Good specimens were highly prized and commanded astonishingly high prices. The cult spread quickly to other resorts which possessed good and varied shingle beaches. Fossiliferous flint pebbles were not the only objects of search. There was frantic rummaging for semi-precious stones. But these deserve a chapter to themselves.

We sometimes find flint pebbles with hollows in them. It is possible that the hollow in the pebble was caused by some irregularity in the deposition of the silica which composed the flint. Small pebbles, washed into the hollow by the tides and eddying round within it, deepened and smoothed it, and now, after the lapse of ages, the finished product of Nature's own grinding and smoothing mill lies on the beach. The better specimens make excellent inkpots and are an ornament to the writing-desk. The Sussex beaches below the chalk cliffs, especially those near Beachy Head, are happy hunting-grounds for the seekers of the deeply hollowed flint pebbles.

We end this chapter with some words of warning against the artificial intruders on the beach. They can masquerade as pebbles and very successfully lead the unsuspecting searcher to think he has made a rare find. The sea washes up on the beaches a medley of flotsam and jetsam, wreckage, fragments of brick and concrete from quays and jetties and pieces of man-made articles borne by rivers into their estuaries. Man himself is no tidier on the beach than he is on Hampstead Heath on a bank holiday. His contribution is also miscellaneous: broken milk bottles, ginger-beer bottles and earthenware galore. The tides treat all these intruders to the beach as they treat the pebbles themselves: they grind them down, knock their corners off, smooth them and eventually bleach them and give them a coating. If the rounding and smoothing has gone on long enough, the deception can be very baffling. It may be less baffling if you keep the following in mind:

1. The pebbles have had a very much longer start in the grinding, rounding and smoothing race, so they all, including even the tough flints, are much more likely to have had their corners rubbed away than the artificial fragments which have been washed up by sea or dropped by man on the beach.

2. You have been advised to use your knife to scrape away the coating from a pebble in order to have a better chance of identifying the rock. The same treatment will enable you to see the true surface of the false pebble. It should quickly unmask any fragment of brick, china or earthenware. As for the two last-mentioned there is no rock in this part of the world that closely resembles them. Some types of earthenware may bear some slight resemblance to very fine sandstone, grit, shale or hard, fine-grained limestone,

but once you have become familiar with the texture of those rocks you are unlikely to mistake a piece of earthenware for a pebble of any one of them. Brick should also be self-revealing. If it is the red variety you recognize it at once. The only rock at all like it in colour is the red sandstone, but, in that rock, the sand-grains are unmistakable. If the brick is the yellow kind, the only rock that bears the slightest resemblance to it is the yellow sandstone and, here again, the sand-grains will emphasize the difference.

Pieces of concrete are much less easily dismissed, because the sand in them may convince you that you have found a pebble of sedimentary rock. If the concrete consists of the usual mixture of cement, sand and gravel you can tell it at once for what it is, but if the gravel is missing from the mixture, as it often is, you may find it harder to distinguish the piece of mortar from a pebble of sandstone or grit. Scratch it vigorously with the point of your knife-blade and examine the powdery stuff that runs into your hand. You are aware that the grains of sandstone and grit are held firmly together by silica and the sand-grains in concrete by cement. The latter was a fine powder before it was mixed up with the sand to form concrete. The knife-scratching will disclose, in each case, the sand-grains, but if the pebble is of concrete, the accompanying powder will be whitish and fine; if it is of sandstone or grit it will be coarser, tougher and more angular. Even so, you cannot be sure. The grains of some sandstones are held together by calcareous cement, which makes them difficult to distinguish from mortar.

3. Glass. A fragment of glass dropped among the shingle and carried up and down by the beach undergoes a curious change. It loses its glassiness or transparency by acquiring a crystalline surface like frosted glass. A piece of an old lemonade bottle of greenish glass that has endured the rolling of thousands of tides takes on a very complete disguise. It has lost its sharp edges and has become a pebble of crystalline beauty. Its greenish tinge adds to its charm and it may beguile its finder into the belief that he has found a semi-precious stone of some rarity, perhaps a pebble of

chrysoberyl or chrysoprase, greenish stones with delectable names. But these are vain hopes. The chances of finding a pebble of either of these stones on a British beach are almost precisely nil. He would not be the first to imagine that a jewel lies at his feet among the shingle. The chrysoprase was a favourite stone in this country in the early nineteenth century for setting in rings and brooches. The lapidaries in Brighton and other fashionable seaside resorts at that time made a brisk sale at high prices of green, crystalline stones that were merely beach-worn fragments of old bottles.

Ordinary colourless glass also has its fascination as a pebble. The quickest and most efficient means of coming to a decision about it is to break off a small piece with your hammer. If it is of glass, its obvious glassiness will be at once apparent. Now there are two rocks of complete, or almost complete, transparency, and you have to decide whether the pebble can be one of those. They are obsidian and pure quartz. Obsidian is a volcanic rock that cooled so quickly after being erupted that it had no chance to crystallize and solidified into glass, but, though there are some glassy rocks in Scotland, they have not the clarity of obsidian and, accordingly, the possibility of finding an obsidian pebble on any of our beaches can be almost entirely discounted. Pure quartz has been known to find its way to a shingle beach, where, in due course, it acquires a frosted appearance. It then looks exactly like a piece of glass that has received the same treatment. You break off a piece. If the quartz is absolutely pure and is a flawless rock crystal (apart from its frosted-looking surface) it will look just like colourless glass, but it will survive a test that glass cannot. Take your sharp piece of flint from your pocket and scratch the glassy surface. If the pebble is quartz, the flint will slide over it and leave it unscratched, because quartz is high up in the scale of hardness. If the flint scratches the pebble, it is glass. There is also another simple test. Strike the pebble hard with the blade of your knife in a dark room. If it emits a spark, accompanied by a slight smell of burning vegetable matter, it is quartz.

Impure quartz, white, opaque and crystalline, appears in pebble form on many of our beaches, but it is easily distinguishable from pebbles of any other rock. Like the common flint, it consists almost wholly of silica. There is a strange fascination about silica. It is to be seen in many guises and the most attractive of these will be the subject of the next chapter, in which we shall discuss semi-precious stones.

IV

THE EXCITING QUEST
FOR SEMI-PRECIOUS STONES

*Some lustrous members of the silica family.
Jet and amber. The lapidary's art*

We hope that this chapter will not stimulate cupidity, raise false hopes or encourage frenzied beach-combing. Let us make it clear at the outset that the beaches of the British Isles yield no truly precious stones. If they did they would have been invaded long ago by hordes of treasure-seekers and our tranquil coast would have witnessed such uproarious scenes as are associated with a Klondyke gold rush. Some very impure and, therefore, almost valueless, sapphires can be found on the Island of Mull, and crystals of topaz were found long ago in Arran, Aberdeenshire and Argyll, but we must remain content with the study of stones that are designated semi-precious. Even they might be more appropriately styled demi-semi-precious.

Nearly all of them consist of silica in one form or another. By far the greater part of the earth's crust consists of silica. We have encountered it already in enormous quantities in the multitude of flint pebbles, in the sandstone, quartz and quartzite pebbles, and in all of those that were formed from igneous rocks. You may think it strange that semi-precious stones consist of such common stuff. The reason is that the silica in these stones has undergone a very slight chemical change that has given them a brilliance and a colouring so different from silica in its cruder state as to transform them. Furthermore, silica possesses some of the virtues that characterize all gems: beauty, durability, hardness and rarity. Clearly, it can claim the second and the third, even in the form of the poor, common flint; the pebbles that we are about to describe can boast of the first; as to the fourth a less substantial claim can be made, but, in searching for semi-precious pebbles among beds of shingle, you may soon convince yourself that they are at least comparatively rare.

As most of the pebbles we shall look at in this chapter are varieties of quartz we can most conveniently consider quartz first and then inspect some of its very pleasing varieties. You already know that quartz is silica itself. It abounds in the sand-grains of every sea-shore and desert and it has obtruded itself into most of the rocks in the earth's surface. We find it in the form of veins in innumerable pebbles, including those of some sedimentary rocks. But, nearly always, it is the white, opaque quartz that is so abundant. The completely transparent, glassy quartz is much rarer. In that form it is commonly known as 'rock-crystal' and often as just 'crystal', a name which originated from the notion that it was petrified ice (Greek: Krustallos = ice). Marbodus, who was Bishop of Rennes in France in the eleventh century, wrote a Latin poem on gems. Here is a translated extract from his description of transparent quartz, which he calls 'crystal':

> *Crystal is ice through countless ages grown*
> *(So teach the wise) to hard transparent stone:*
> *And still the gem retains its native force,*
> *And holds the cold and colour of its source.*
> *Yet some deny, and tell of crystal found*
> *Where never icy winter froze the ground.*

Some confusion exists even to-day in the minds of some pebble-collectors over the clear and the opaque kinds of quartz. They persist in calling the former 'crystal' and the latter 'quartz', whereas, of course, both are quartz.

Do not expect to find large pebbles of entirely pure, transparent quartz on the beach. They are usually small and, as you have learned in the last chapter, are likely to have a frosted appearance, so that scraping, and, perhaps, breaking, will be necessary to secure identification. To find the really flawless specimens you will have to travel to Brazil. The perfect quartz crystal takes the form of a six-sided (hexagonal) prism with a six-sided pyramid at each end. The shape varies and the hexagon is sometimes irregular.

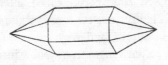

FIGURE 9

Waste no time in looking for such a prize. You must be content with small, fragmental pieces. Remember the hardness test and so make sure that you are not carrying home a piece of bottle-glass.

Now let us look at some of the varieties or relatives of quartz. Together they make up a most attractive family.

Amethyst, or amethystine quartz, is the transparent rock-crystal quartz with a light purple or violet colour, due probably to the presence in the stone of some of the element, manganese. A cut and polished pebble of amethyst is a joy to behold and to possess. Good specimens were valuable about 150 years ago, but the price fell heavily when Germany imported large quantities of them into this country. Careful search can occasionally reveal the pebbles on some of the Cornish beaches. They also appear on the east coast of Scotland, whence some of them are carried by longshore drifting to the beaches of the north-east coast of England.

Rose Quartz, unlike amethyst, is not a variety of the transparent, but of the common opaque quartz. Even so, it is a very attractive pink stone and the pebbles are worthy of their place in a collector's cabinet. Just as opaque quartz is much commoner than the clear rock crystal, so rose quartz is less rare than amethyst. The pink colouring is attributed to the presence of the metal titanium.

Citrine, or yellow quartz, is, like amethyst, a variety of the clear rock-crystal quartz. The colour varies from lemon-yellow to golden. This gives the stone some resemblance to the gem, topaz, and it is often sold under the label of Scotch topaz, occidental topaz or fake topaz, thereby fetching a higher price than yellow quartz could command.

Smoky Quartz, or Cairngorm, called after the Cairngorm Mountains in Scotland, from the massive granite of which they were extracted, is another, and very attractive, variety of rock-crystal quartz. Its colour ranges from yellow through deep orange to dark brown and it is accompanied by a smokiness that seems to lend added beauty to the lustre of the cut and polished pebble. The stones are familiar to all as the ornaments of Highland dress. The pebbles find their way to Scottish beaches and reach the east coast of England in course of time by longshore drifting. A good specimen is a joy to the lapidary. The more yellow kind, like citrine, is not unlike topaz, but it lacks the hardness and the heaviness of that gem.

Chalcedony (pronounced 'Kal-sed-onni', with the stress on the second syllable) takes its name from Chalcedon in Asia Minor. It is non-crystalline, translucent quartz with a milky blue-grey or pale brown tinge and a waxiness of lustre, but its chief characteristic is its extraordinary form. Its surface is raised in rounded lumps suggestive of a bunch of grapes or a collection of soap-bubbles, an arrangement technically known as concretionary or botryoidal (Greek: botrus = a bunch of grapes). When broken, chalcedony is seen to be of a fibrous structure. Extremely thin fibres that look like hairs radiate out from the centre of each rounded lump to its surface.

The ancient Babylonians, Persians, Etruscans, Greeks and Romans made much use of the stone for sculpture and ornamentation and it was in much demand for signet-rings. These had the reputation of bringing to their wearers good luck in their litigation. The poem from which we have already quoted says of chalcedony:

> *But pierced and worn upon the neck or hand*
> *A sure success in lawsuits 'twill command.*

Yet, so slight is the difference in composition between chalcedony and the poor, common flint, that the latter may be said to be just an inferior form of it. It would be equally true to say that the other varieties of silica that we are about to examine differ only in very slight degree from chalcedony.

You must not expect to find good specimens of it without prolonged search, for it is considerably rarer than quartz. It originates from cavities in granite and other igneous rocks and sometimes in the Old Red Sandstones. Good specimens are found on the Scottish coast and on the eastern and southern coasts of England.

The remaining varieties of quartz that we shall look at resemble chalcedony so much in all but colour and surface-form that they might well be, and often are, called varieties of chalcedony. They are Agate, Onyx, Carnelian and Sard. All, like chalcedony, are non-crystalline and translucent forms of quartz. The cut and polished pebbles are charming, but you should take only your best specimens to the lapidary, as they are all harder than the most highly tempered steel and put up a stiff resistance to his cutting apparatus.

Of the several kinds of Agate (Latin: Achates = a river in Sicily) we can give our attention to the three that are the choicest and most striking.

Banded or striped agate is so called because its cut surface exhibits a succession of curved bands, stripes or layers, each band differing in colour from its neighbours. The curves are very roughly concentric and all of them are parallel to one another. Overleaf is a simple plan of the structure of banded agate on the cut surface of a pebble.

Agates came into existence in the cavities of igneous rocks in much the same way as flint is usually formed in the hollows of chalk

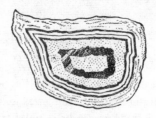

FIGURE 10

—that is, by the solidifying of liquid silica in the cavities. But in the case of agate, the solution of silica did not fill the cavity and then solidify. There appear to have been several stages in the process, separated by some intervals of time. It is this that accounts for the difference in colouring of the layers. The first solution that poured into the cavity may have been pure silica, which solidified into colourless quartz, and the second may have contained a chemical which coloured it, and so on. The effect of this process is most charmingly revealed on the cut and polished surface of a banded agate pebble.

Sometimes the concentric banding takes the shape of the ground-plan of a fortress, the bands being more angular than curved and suggesting the bastions and salients in the fortress wall. A stone with banding of such a pattern is aptly called Fortification Agate. Note from the illustration (Plate 24) the cut surface of a pebble of this variety. Note also the rough, uncut surface of the pebble. The very great difference between the two should convince you that some of your choicest finds can have unpromising exteriors.

You will also observe that the banding is roughly parallel to the outer surface of the pebble and must consequently have been parallel to the walls of the cavity filled by the stone. This is not always so. It happens to be so in this particular pebble because it had had few of its corners rubbed off. Many agate pebbles have been so rounded that the banding has disappeared here and there from the surface.

Our third kind is Moss Agate. It contains no moss at all or, indeed, any other vegetable matter. The mossy-looking filaments that give it its name result from the infiltration of some inorganic material, possibly oxide of manganese. Their ramifications through the translucent silica, in which they seem to float, give the stone an enchanting appearance and make it the acknowledged favourite of many collectors.

Banded agates, though not common, are present in sufficient numbers on many of our beaches to reward a patient but not arduous search. Perhaps their highest frequency is on some parts of the Scottish coast, where agates of alternating pink and white bands have long been known as 'Scotch pebbles'. On the east coast of England there are good specimens at Scarborough, Filey, Cromer, Aldeburgh, Felixstowe, Ramsgate and Deal. Many beaches on the south coast are also productive, but the best of the hunting-grounds between Dover and Land's End is the Cornish coast. The biggest and best agates come from other parts of the world. They abound so much in Brazil and Uruguay that it used to be customary to load them into ships as ballast and to transport them from those countries to Germany to be cut and polished. That process went on in and around a town called Oberstein, where a huge trade in agate-working had been established, the grinding mills being driven by bountiful water-power. Magnificent slabs of agate are cut and polished there for export throughout the world and for conversion into ornaments of every description. Commercial agate, however, must not be accepted at face value. The dull banding of some of the stones is artificially brightened by heating, staining and treatment with acids. The secrets of the agate-staining racket were known many centuries ago to Italian jewellers. In the last century they were passed on to the agate-workers of Oberstein and the practice still continues.

You will find far more joy in the small and modest agate pebble you have found on one of the home beaches, cut and polished by a local lapidary, than in any of the huge, coruscating, multi-coloured slabs from Oberstein.

Onyx, an equally lovely stone, we can dismiss in a few lines. Imagine a banded agate in which the bands are straight, not curved: that is onyx. The stone lends itself admirably to the cutting of cameos. It is much rarer than banded agate and is consequently more valuable. The cameo-worker prefers the onyx of alternating black and white bands so that the figure he cuts on the white band can stand out against the background of black. You will be fortunate indeed to find an onyx pebble of clearly defined banding. You are more likely to discover a cloudy specimen with its black shading off into white through gradations of grey. This is a much less attractive stone than the commoner banded agate.

Be on your guard against the assumption that any pebble that contains straight bands must be an onyx. Innumerable pebbles of the commoner kinds contain straight bands of quartz. Slate and schist often have such banding. If you are in any doubt, apply the simple knife-blade test to the parts of the pebble that lie between the white bands. The blade will easily scratch the slate or schist pebble. It will make no impression upon any part of one that is onyx or agate.

Carnelian, formerly called Cornelian (Latin: cornu = horn) on account of its horny appearance, underwent a change of name in comparatively recent times, perhaps because carnelian, supposedly derived from the Latin, carneus = flesh-coloured, is more truly descriptive of it. It is a very beautiful stone, regarded as the purest form of chalcedony and assessed by some collectors as more attractive than the agate. Very often it has a flesh tint, but the colour can range from yellow, through brown to red. The red variety is often confused with jasper (which we shall discuss later) by people who are unaware that jasper is completely opaque and carnelian is translucent. If you hold up a pebble of reddish carnelian to a strong light, even though it is very beach-worn and coated, you will see a delightful, roseate glow within it. Pebbles that have red speckles are not carnelian but an impure kind of chalcedony. Good specimens of carnelian must be of uniform colour and wholly translucent. The deep, clear red variety responds best of all to the lapidary's skill. It was highly esteemed in ancient Rome and must have been still much in favour in the eleventh century, for, to quote Marbodus again:

> Let not the Muse the dull cornelian slight
> Although it shine with but a feeble light;
> Fate has with virtues great its nature grac'd.
> Tied round the neck or on the finger plac'd,
> Its friendly influence checks the rising fray
> And chases spites and quarrels far away.

The pebbles are found on some beaches on the east coast of Scotland, and on the coasts of Cornwall, the Isle of Wight, Kent, especially near Deal, Yorkshire and Suffolk. The Felixstowe and Cromer beaches have yielded many good specimens.

In your search for carnelians or any other pebbles of translucent stone you should adopt a technique different from the one recommended in the previous chapter for 'beach-combing' of a more general kind. Select that strip of shingle from which the tide has very recently receded and walk very slowly along it with the sun right in front of you, keeping your eyes on the pebbles a yard or two ahead of you. If a carnelian is peeping out from among its more commonplace companions, its translucent quality will be just sufficient to draw your gaze towards it. But, you may object, one cannot order the movements of the sun to coincide with one's visits to the beach in such a way as to ensure this method of search. Obviously not. Everything depends on the orientation of the beach and the time of the visit. But, given all the favourable conditions, you can take advantage of them.

Commercial carnelian does not always live up to its description. The fleshy redness of the natural carnelian is due to the presence of iron oxide in the stone. It can be artificially created by staining or by treating the stone with a solution of one of the salts of iron and then heating it.

The last of the translucent members of the quartz family that calls for notice here is Sard. It is really a variety of carnelian, but it is harder, tougher, of richer colour, of more uniform quality and of brighter lustre than ordinary carnelian. Hence it is more valuable. Sard of the choicest kind is said to possess the rare quality of chatoyance. This word (derived from the French: chat = cat) means the changing of colour in the lustre as the stone is moved around in the light. The similar behaviour of cats' eyes in the darkness doubtless gave rise to the term. The peculiar toughness of sard also enhances the value of the stone. Very ancient specimens retain a smooth and bright surface long after harder and more precious gems show signs of wear.

You will be fortunate indeed to find one, but, having found one, you will find it hard to distinguish it from carnelian, as the two stones are of the same chemical composition—that is, chalcedony coloured by iron oxide—and they shade off, one into the other. It is impossible to draw precisely a border-line between the two.

Before we leave the subject of chalcedonic quartz pebbles we must refer to one more variety, not because you are ever likely to discover one, but because its name is a compound of two that we have already considered and may consequently be confusing to you unless its nature is now made clear. This is the Sardonyx. It is by far the most valuable member of the chalcedony family. It probably acquired this name because it is a fusion of certain qualities of the sard and the onyx. In its straight, parallel banding it is an onyx, but one or more of the bands consist of sard or carnelian. The bands are white and either brown or red. Exquisite specimens come from India and Arabia to be cut into seals and cameos. There has always been a brisk trade in imitation sardonyx, produced by the chemical treatment of cheap Brazilian agate or inferior carnelian. Only an expert gemmologist can detect the difference between the genuine and the imitation stone.

And now for a look at Jasper, an opaque variety of quartz. It is very much commoner on the beaches than its translucent relatives and is almost valueless, being an inferior form of quartz, but it has a charm of its own to the pebble-collector. He appreciates it for its colour and its hardness. The colour is usually a dull red, but it is sometimes brown or yellowish-green. One or other of the salts of iron is responsible for the colouring. If you break a pebble of jasper, the fresh fracture will reveal through your pocket lens a multitude of tiny quartz grains mingled with material that looks like dried clay. In fact, it is clay. But for its presence the pebble would consist of pure quartz. The admixture of the clay has made it impure and completely opaque. The point of your knife will make a faint mark on the surface of the jasper pebble and, as you know, would make no impression upon it if it were quartz.

You should not dismiss the jasper with contempt because of its impurity and opaqueness. The polished pebble will look well in your collection. If you chance to find a pebble of conglomerate in which fragments of jasper are intermingled with those of quartz, snatch it eagerly. A polished slice of it would grace your cabinet, for it resembles a superlative piece of inlaid work.

Jasper pebbles are to be found on so many of our beaches that a list of localities would be superfluous. On some Yorkshire and Devonshire beaches you may find some very pleasingly striped varieties. These are stones that lie midway between the jasper and the agate. They provide a reminder to us that all the varieties of quartz have no clear lines of demarcation. They tend to merge one into another. The Bloodstone, sometimes called the Heliotrope, is another variety of jasper and is much less frequently encountered than the ordinary red jasper pebble. Its colouring is a rich green, mottled with blood-red spots. This vividly contrasting combination gives it a singular beauty, which becomes resplendent when the stone is cut and polished. Good specimens are a little less opaque than ordinary jasper and this slight translucency enhances their charm. The word 'heliotrope' suggests to us the purple tint of the flowers called by that name, but it applied originally to certain tropical flowers that turned with the sun, being derived from the Greek words meaning 'sun' and 'I turn'. It must have been given to the stone because of the popular belief that the image of the sun turned to the colour of blood when one looked at its reflection in the stone.

Here we must leave quartz and all its relatives that together comprise the fascinating silica family. In parting from them we must take the risk of becoming wearisome and offer a few words of advice to those who are eager to seek them on the beach.

Firstly, bear always in mind that pebbles of these lovely stones do not reveal themselves to the casual beach wanderer, for, like all other beach pebbles, they have endured the rolling of the tides, the bleaching of sun and wind and the coating that all pebbles acquire in course of time. At first you will experience disappointment even on the beaches reputed to have a high content of the semi-precious varieties of silica; but on the second, or perhaps the third, day of patient searching, you will suddenly become aware with a delicious thrill that you have gained the knack of piercing the disguises of the chalcedonic pebbles. Thenceforward your progress will be rapid and joyous.

Secondly, the beaches specifically mentioned in the foregoing paragraphs as being well stocked with these pebbles are not the only parts of the coast which could reward your search for them. Not many beds of shingle are completely devoid of them. The least promising beaches are those in deep bays guarded by long headlands, which set up a formidable barrier against longshore drifting. But even here your search will not be in vain if the cliffs at the back of the beach are of igneous or metamorphic rocks or if they are surmounted by a layer of boulder clay. The unproductive beach is the closely guarded one on a coast backed by cliffs of limestone or shale.

Thirdly, the modern nomenclature of the semi-precious stones differs, in some respects, from the old and can cause some bewilderment to those who are unaware of the changes. The peoples of old used the names of their ornamental stones rather loosely, so, if you come upon a passage in biblical or classical literature referring to a stone in terms contradictory to those used in this chapter, do not begin to wonder whether you have been misled. Here, for instance, is a reference to jasper, which we know to be opaque:

'And her light was like unto a stone most precious, even like a jasper stone, clear as crystal.' (Revelation, xxi, 11.) Obviously, the jasper was the name of one of the precious and completely transparent stones at the time when those words were written.

Now we must look at two stones that have originated from the vegetable kingdom. Their distribution on our coast is somewhat local, but they are of sufficient interest, value and appearance to merit some attention. They are Jet and Amber.

Jet is a very close relative of coal, especially of lignite (wood-coal), bituminous coal and anthracite, but it is much harder and glossier and possesses the qualities that entitle it to rank as an ornamental stone. A thin slice of it shows that it has a woody texture and it might be designated as wood, decomposed, fossilized or bituminized, yet all the softness of the woody fibres has gone and, like any other stone, jet sinks in water.

A polished pebble of good-quality jet is of midnight black with a brilliant lustre, caressingly smooth to the touch, of light weight and entirely opaque. Inferior jet is black with a tinge of brown and is a little softer. The only substantial deposits of jet in Great Britain are at Whitby on the Yorkshire coast, in that same formation of shale as occur the ammonites or snake-stones to which we have referred in the last chapter. It is strange that no jet is found in other parts of the country where shale abounds and where huge accumulations of the decomposed wood of ancient forests have caused the formation of coal-seams.

The biggest mass of it occurs in a cliff appropriately named the Jet Rock. The layer runs inland for a considerable distance. Long ago the task of the jet-workers was easy. They had only to roam the beach and pick up lumps of it. These lumps were parts of the residue of cliffs broken down by the attacking waves. When that supply became exhausted, the jet-workers had to drive galleries into the cliffs and sink shafts inland. Meanwhile the longshore drifting, which, on this coast, as you should remember, is from north to south, carried many of the jet pebbles down the east coast. Some of them are still picked up many miles south of Whitby.

Jet began to be fashionable in the Bronze Age. The burrows or graves of that prehistoric era have yielded bracelets, rings, beads, necklaces and other ornaments of jet. Roman literature contains references to the bountiful supply of jet in Britain and numerous ornaments carved from it have been excavated from the sites of villas and garrison towns inhabited by the Romans during their long occupation of this country. The source of all of them was probably Whitby, where the jet-workers can surely boast of being engaged in one of the oldest, if not the very oldest, trade in Great Britain. Whitby jet was high in the list of British exports to the Continent in the Middle Ages. We have since imported jet from Spain and France, but it is softer and less glossy than the Whitby product. There are numerous imitations, including Pennsylvania anthracite, bituminous coal, black glass, black obsidian and chalcedony stained black. The feminine demand for jet ornaments fluctuates. They were much in vogue with our grandmothers and great-grandmothers, who delighted in jet necklaces and fringes adorned with jet beads.

If you find on the east coast a pebble that you think is jet, you can easily make sure of it. Scrape the surface to reveal the dense blackness, hardness and glossiness. Test its weight. It should be very light. If it is not lighter than a piece of glass of the same size, it is not jet. To make quite sure, break off a piece and hold it in the flame of a match. It should burn with a greenish flame and give off a pleasant smell, sweet and suggestive of tar. There is supposed to be another test, which, so far, the author has not had the courage to apply, alluring though it is. Pour oil on the burning jet and it will quench the flame, but pour water on it and you will have a crackling conflagration.

Occasionally and erroneously jet is called black amber, because it possesses, though only to a slight extent, the property of becoming electrified by vigorous rubbing and of attracting small objects as a magnet attracts iron filings.

And this leads us to the second of our two stones of vegetable origin, Amber, known to the ancient world as electron, from which we get our word electricity. Most schoolboys have seen their science master rub a piece of amber on cloth and then hold it over a pile of little scraps of paper, whereupon the scraps fly up to the amber and cling to it.

Strictly speaking, amber is not a stone. It consists of fossil resin. In the remote past the liquid resin bubbled out of pine-trees, now long extinct, in forests of vast extent, stretching from the Baltic to the Mediterranean. The hardened fossilized resin was washed by the waves out into the Baltic Sea, the biggest deposits being off the coast of Pomerania. When the liquid amber exuded from the trees and dropped on the ground it gathered up a motley collection of fragments and slowly solidified around them. It entombed within itself gnats, flies, spiders and beetles and numerous little creatures that then inhabited the trunks of pine trees. Their fossilized remains, clearly visible in the amber, present an enthralling study to entomologists, especially because they are unlike the insects now inhabiting northern Europe and resemble those that now exist in more southern, and therefore warmer, latitudes.

The deposits of amber in the Baltic were rolled along, as the centuries passed, into the North Sea and by infinitely slow stages to our east coast. Pieces of it are still being picked up on the beaches between Yorkshire and Essex, especially at Cromer, Yarmouth, Southwold, Aldeburgh and Felixstowe. If you are fortunate enough to find one, you can quickly make up your mind about it. The colour varies from pale primrose to deep orange. It is the softest of all the stones we have mentioned, being only a little harder than rock-salt, which can be scratched with the finger-nail, and a knife-blade will therefore make a deep impression in amber. It is also brittle and, like jet, is light in weight and burns in a match flame. The colour of the flame is yellow and the odour it emits is aromatic. Of course, the most convincing of tests is to tear up a small sheet of paper into pieces, rub the amber on your sleeve and watch its effect upon the pieces of paper when you hold it above them. Do not expect to find any pieces larger than a small nut. One extremely lucky person found on the Suffolk coast, over a hundred years ago, a large block of it weighing thirteen pounds and of an estimated value of £4,500. We hesitate to suggest what sum a block of that size would command in the currency of to-day, but you should think twice before rushing to Suffolk in the hope of finding a replica of it and of thus ensuring an immediate and comfortable retirement.

For personal ornamentation amber has been in demand in Europe since the late Stone Age. We know that amber ornaments were in vogue in Britain in the Bronze Age, because they have been found here in tombs of that period, but it is in the East that amber has been most highly prized. Great quantities have been exported from the German shores of the Baltic to Constantinople, Egypt, Arabia, India and Persia, there to be fashioned into ornaments of all descriptions. It was, and still is, frequently carved into mouth-pieces for pipes. The hookah-smokers of Turkey regarded it almost with veneration, for in that country it was thought to be a complete safeguard against infection. As it was the courteous custom to offer a guest in a Turkish household a pull at the family hookah, he could enjoy his smoke without fear of inhaling any of the bacilli that his hosts might have been entertaining unawares.

It is time now to leave the semi-precious stones and to visit the workshop of the lapidary to see how he does the cutting and polishing to which we have made such frequent reference. These processes, especially when applied to the very hard stones such as chalcedony and its varieties, are long and arduous, so you should select only the very best of your specimens for his attention. Pebbles of the less refractory kind are cut fairly easily and, consequently, less expensively.

The cutting and the polishing of gems have been going on for over 4,500 years. Egyptian lapidaries were cutting scarab seals and those of Assyria and Babylonia cylindrical seals at least as early as 2500 B.C. They did it by hand or with the most primitive of instruments. The story of the developments, and also the setbacks, in the art through the thousands of subsequent years is very engaging, but this is not the place for its narration. We must enter the workshop of the twentieth-century lapidary. In London he will be found at work in the Hatton Garden district, the centre of the jewellery and gem-cutting trades. If you live in London and take your pebbles home for treatment, you must make your way there, but you may find the lapidaries too busily engaged in gem-cutting to bother about your pebbles. If you cannot wait for the end of your holiday and happen to be spending it at one of the larger seaside resorts which have beaches that yield interesting pebbles, the local lapidary's shop, usually near the beach, invites your custom. You may be sure that he is familiar with that beach and you should certainly take his advice upon the choice of your stones for cutting. Occasionally he is to be found at the smaller seaside places, where the shingle is unusually rich in attractive pebbles: the Cornish coast, for instance, which is an El Dorado for the pebble-collector.

Having entered, you will want to stay, not only to see the fascinating operations he performs on the pebbles, but also to gaze at the fashioned stones awaiting delivery. In both the processes of cutting and polishing the hard pebbles of semi-precious stone, the lapidary works with discs. For cutting he uses the rim of a steel disc; for polishing he uses the flat surface of another disc. In other words, the first wheel or disc cuts by its edge, the second polishes by its surface.

All but the very hard stones are cut with comparative ease with saws of tempered steel. Granite, for instance, is dealt with in this way. The expression 'hard as granite' must have been put into circulation by a person who knew nothing of mineralogy, for, though granite seems hard to the touch, it is soft in comparison with flint, jasper and the varieties of chalcedonic quartz. To cut them the lapidary uses a disc of *soft* steel. Why a soft disc for such hard stones? Well, a pebble of agate or jasper would quickly wear out the teeth of the most highly tempered saw, but it will not easily wear out a steel rim soft enough to have diamond dust embedded in it. Diamond stands at the top of the hardness scale for minerals.[1] Mixed with oil into a paste it is rubbed into the rim of the soft steel wheel, which has first been scarified by the lapidary's knife. The diamond dust lodges in the scratches and enormously reinforces the steel rim of the electrically driven wheel. Indeed, it imparts to the rim an adamantine hardness, for diamond is adamant—that is, a stone of impenetrable hardness.

After the pebble has been cut in two, you or the lapidary (preferably the latter) must decide whether either of the cut surfaces is worthy of being polished. There will be some little difference between them, because a section as thick as the disc has been cut out from between them. Before the polishing process begins it may be necessary to remove some little scars or notches which the cutting operation has left on the surface. The lapidary grinds the surface down to completely even flatness by pressing the pebble down on a disc of lead or copper, having first spread on the disc a paste of fine grains of emery. Emery is a variety of carborundum, which comes next in the scale of hardness to the diamond. The grains become embedded in the rotating wheel and quickly remove the irregularities. Polishing then begins. It usually consists of two operations. The first one is conducted on a wooden disc (sometimes on one of leather) on which powdered pumice stone has been scattered. The final one, which imparts the high, gleaming polish, is done on a wheel made of felt, the polishing medium being rotten stone, otherwise called tripolite or tripoli powder, a sandy, friable earth of a greyish-white colour. Sometimes the lapidary employs a chemical preparation for this final polish. If the interior of your pebble has fulfilled your expectations, whether in richness of colour, delicacy or intricacy of pattern or attractiveness of its fossilized contents, you will be delighted with the lustrous sheen that the lapidary's polishing has given to it.

Do not forget to take back with you the other half of your

[1] You may well ask: if a diamond is to be cut, what mineral is hard enough to cut it? The answer is another diamond. The fact that diamond cuts diamond was revealed in the fifteenth century.

pebble to take its place in your collection as the fellow of the polished piece. The latter you will display, of course, with its polished surface uppermost; the former with its cut surface downwards. It is most desirable to show the polished surface in juxtaposition with the rough, weathered surface of the same stone, not only to provide a striking contrast, but to help you to keep in mind what a pebble of this particular kind looks like on the beach. You will be pleasantly surprised to find how greatly this will facilitate your future searches among the shingle.

Some fervent pebble-collectors, gifted with mechanical knowledge, unlimited patience and manual dexterity, set up their own workshops and spend gratifying winter evenings in fashioning the pebbles they have hoarded in the summer. Lacking all these enviable qualities, we have not ventured to follow their enterprising example and we counsel you to be equally unresourceful, unless, of course, you are a mechanical genius. The usual rewards of the amateur lapidary are lacerated fingers, splinters of stone in the eyes, mutilated pebbles and a wasteful expenditure of diamond dust.

If you fail to secure the services of a lapidary, or if you cannot go to the trouble of finding one, you may perhaps find some satisfaction in the following cheap and easy method of giving your pebbles a polished appearance.

Just as a clean, wet pebble displays a clearer surface than a dry one, so a clean, varnished pebble reveals a surface at least as clear and retains it for a much longer period. While the sheen of the varnish lasts, the pebble almost appears to have been polished. You can also apply the varnish to a flattened side of a pebble. All limestones, for example, and many other rocks that are not high on the scale of hardness, rub down easily on a flat piece of tough sandstone or grit. A smoother polish may be obtained on a flat piece of carborundum, and a still better one by using different grades of carborundum powder on a piece of plate glass.

V

THE COASTLINE OF ENGLAND AND WALES

Its pebble-beaches and what to look for on them

We shall now make a rapid tour of the English and Welsh coasts, most regretfully omitting those of Scotland. The deep indentations of the Scottish coastline give it a length out of all proportion to the size of the country and a description of it, even in bare outline, is outside the scope of this book. This is all the more to be deplored, because so much of the coast of Scotland is unsurpassed in grandeur and charm. It most certainly deserves a book to itself.

Let us start at Berwick-on-Tweed and make our way down the east coast of England, along the south coast to Land's End and up the west coast to the Solway Firth, pausing here and there to look more closely at the beaches which bear pebbles of unusual interest and hastening along those of little merit.

A pebble connoisseur, who roamed the English beaches over a century ago in search of semi-precious and fossiliferous stones, made this pronouncement: 'Mediocrity in pebbles is insufferable.' We do not go so far as that. Every pebble is of some interest, but there are a few beaches where the pebbles are so uniform in nature as to damp the ardour of the most fervent collector. These we will pass over rapidly.

(A) THE EAST COAST: BERWICK-ON-TWEED TO DOVER

The Northumberland coast has much to offer the student of

pebbles and also gives him a pleasant setting for the pursuit of his hobby. Its attractiveness lies in its long, sandy bays, Holy Island, the Farne Islands archipelago, and the expansive sand-dunes in the bays north of Dunstanburgh Castle.

The prevailing rocks in the low-lying land behind the beaches are shale and limestone and they, of course, have made a large contribution to the shingle, but other sources have added their quota and, together, they make up an inviting miscellany. All this region received a thick covering of glacial drift during the Ice Age and there are few parts of its coast where layers of boulder clay are not exposed. The shingle, in consequence, contains innumerable pebbles that have made long, glacier-borne journeys, many of them from the distant north and all of them setting you a pretty little problem as to their origin and content. Then, again, the river Tweed, fed by tributaries from the hills of southern Scotland, has rolled down to its estuary at Berwick the pebbles it has shaped during its long, meandering course. The longshore drifting from north to south has brought many of them to the Northumbrian beaches. It has also brought pebbles from the coast of Berwickshire, products of the fine-grained red volcanic rocks that form the impressive St. Abb's Head and of the medley of igneous and sedimentary cliffs still farther north. Another most interesting source of the shingle is a formation of rock known to geologists as the Great Whin Sill. A sill is an intrusive sheet of igneous rock between the layers (or bedding-planes) of older rocks. At the time of the intrusion the invading rock must have been in a liquid or semi-liquid state and, as it slowly cooled and solidified, it took the shape of the space into which it had obtruded itself. We have used the word 'sheet', which suggests a layer of extreme thinness, but the Great Whin Sill has an average thickness of 100 feet. However, even this is thin enough in comparison with the length and breadth of the sill, for it has pushed its way into five counties: Northumberland, Durham, Yorkshire, Cumberland and Westmorland, its penetrations covering an area of 1,500 square miles. The rock is hard and durable, standing out here and there in ridges above the softer sedimentary rocks which have been less able to resist denudation. One of these ridges is the long one on which the Roman Hadrian built his wall. Another gives a firm foundation to the walls of Bamburgh and Dunstanburgh castles. The Farne Islands are made of it. It comes out on the coast at Budle Point and in the Harkness Rocks, east of Bamburgh Castle, then almost disappears, appearing prominently again in the form of a fairly high cliff at Dunstanburgh and running thence all the way to Cullernose Point. Here you will notice clearly the columnar formation of the Whin rock. The columns are much less regular in shape than the hexagonal columns of basalt on the Isle of Staffa. Most of them are very roughly pentagonal (five-sided). The Whin Sill rock cooled too slowly to become basalt. It can be more correctly termed dolerite. Whinstone pebbles deserve a place in your collection. Break one of them and examine the surface of the fresh fracture. Its colour, in most instances, is a dark greyish-blue. Its crystals are smaller than those of granite, which took longer to cool.

The only trace of the Whinstone on Holy Island (Lindisfarne) is the piece of rock on which the castle stands. The rest of the island is of sedimentary rock, most of it sandstone. You will find many sandstone pebbles among the shingle of the island; intermingled with them are some pebbles of the boulder clay in which this coast abounds.

Proceeding southwards from Cullernose Point, we pass along a coast of shale, sandstone and grit. Millstone grit is the predominant rock for most of the way to Alnmouth and beyond that estuary to the mouth of the river Coquet. The shingle spits on the northern side of each of these estuaries clearly show that the longshore drift of pebbles all along this coast is from north to south. In each case the accumulation of the southward drifting shingle has prevented the river from entering the sea at a more northerly point. The shingle consists of grit and sandstone pebbles, together with the many varieties of ice-borne pebbles eroded from the boulder clay. It may save wearisome repetition if we state here

102

that layers of boulder clay extend with but few interruptions as far south as the Wash. We shall mention the other rocks as we progress southwards to the Norfolk coast, but not boulder clay, unless it happens to be of exceptional interest. Meanwhile, please remember that, wherever there is shingle on this long stretch of coast, it must contain many long-travelled pebbles that the waves have washed out of the clay.

Sand-dunes and headlands of hard sandstone are the prominent features of the coast between the mouth of the Coquet and Tyne-mouth, but industrialization has almost ruined its former beauty. It also mars most of the Durham coast. The section between the Tyne estuary and Hartlepool possesses features of unique interest. These are the cliffs of magnesian limestone, a variety of limestone containing magnesium carbonate and of a yellow colour. The Dolomites, the mountain range in the Southern Tyrol, are made of this stone. Hence it is sometimes called dolomitic limestone. It is hard and crystalline, but the battering effect of the waves upon cliffs of this kind of limestone produces curious effects. It cuts capes and arches in it, and fringes the coast with stacks or islets. These features are seen to the best advantage in Marsden Bay. Where there is shingle on the magnesian limestone coast it contains, of course, numerous pebbles of that stone. Their texture, especially that of freshly broken pebbles, is attractive. It displays a fine-grained, yet crystalline, mosaic. The other components of the shingle are pebbles of sandstone, grit, shale and whinstone brought by southward drifting from the Northumbrian shore and ice-borne pebbles from Cumberland, Northumberland, Scotland and Scandinavia.

Industry has brought to the Durham coast, not only the unsightliness which seems to be its inevitable accompaniment, but also two alien and unpleasing deposits. There are dumps of ballast between Crimden and Hartlepool; at Easington waste material from the collieries has been pitched over the cliffs, despoiling the beach below and blackening the beaches to the south, whither the longshore drifting remorselessly carries the rubbish.

We come now to the long coastline of Yorkshire, which has some impressive cliff scenery and many beaches attractive to the pebble-collector. Cliffs of rock do not appear until we pass south of Saltburn, then shale cliffs rise to commanding heights. In the lovely sweep of Runswick Bay is an interesting beach, but the coast beyond Kettleness is not exciting until we approach Whitby. We have already referred to Whitby at some length, firstly in connection with the ammonites in its shale rocks, and then with the jet for which it is famous. A hard shale promontory called Saltwick Nab lies to the east of Whitby, and from this point a fine line of cliffs, shale and sandstone, extends to Robin Hood's Bay, a glorious sweep between magnificent headlands. About three miles to the south there are good pebbles in the little bay of Hayburn Wyke.

We are now approaching Scarborough along cliffs of oolitic limestone and sandstone, but the rocks are hidden for much of the way by boulder clay. The hard sandstone headland jutting out from Scarborough offers a stiff resistance to the erosive powers of the waves, but it contributes many pebbles to Scarborough's lovely beaches. So do the other rocks of the district: shale, limestone and grit. Scarborough is one of the haunts of the inveterate pebble-collector. He finds here an assortment that should satisfy the most persistent, for, in addition to the pebbles formed from the local rocks and the abundant glacial drift, there are many that have travelled southwards from Scotland, Northumberland and Durham. All the sedimentary rocks that we have noted on our passage from Berwick-on-Tweed produce many fossil-bearing pebbles and there are not a few agates, carnelians, and other members of the translucent silica family.

The next beach of interest is Filey Bay, protected on the north by Filey Brigg, a fine promontory composed of grit. The rock of the cliffs that line the bay is oolitic limestone, but most of it is hidden by huge masses of boulder clay. The barrier of Filey Brigg holds up the southward drifting of pebbles from the north, but they make their way round in time, so the shingle of Filey Bay is varied and well repays a visit.

We are now on the verge of a huge expanse of chalk country. About four miles south of Filey fine, white chalk appears. It forms a range of chalk cliffs all the way to Flamborough Head and thence on to Sewerby. Chalk is almost always accompanied by layers and nodules of flint. One of the rare exceptions is the line of cliffs south of Flamborough Head. They are free from flint. Those on the north, however, are flint-bearing. Look out at Sewerby for a raised beach, formed before the Ice Age altered the shore level. It lies between the boulder clay and the chalk.

From Sewerby, where the chalk disappears, just south of Flamborough Head, to the Wash, there are some eighty miles of coast. Behind it, the chalk runs back into Yorkshire and Lincolnshire for miles, but on it no chalk is to be seen. The beaches are backed almost entirely by boulder clay. It is a coastline which shows most markedly the effects of the Ice Age and also the erosive effects of the tides upon shores unprotected by hard rocks. Flintless chalk puts up little resistance to the waves, because no shingle beds of flint pebbles accumulate below the cliffs to form a defensive barrier. There is geological evidence that the tides had severely eroded the soft chalk before the glaciers covered the coast with thick layers of boulder clay. This also is subject to erosion, but the multitude of pebbles it contains helps to form a beach, which gives some defence against the tides. Nevertheless, it has been estimated that in the last 1,500 years the sea has gained on the land from Sewerby to Spurn Head to a depth of 1½ miles. The list of lost towns on this coast is of melancholy length. Erosion still goes on. In the latter half of the nineteenth century it went on at the rate of nearly two yards per annum.

The longshore drifting of beach material to the south between Flamborough Head and Spurn Head is unusually rapid. There is comparatively little shingle on the beaches. The waves carry it quickly down the Holderness coast to Spurn Head, where, with sand, it forms a spit about three miles long pointing in a S.S.E. direction. The growth of this long nose has been rapid and the Spurn Head lighthouse at its tip has often had to be moved.

Much of the beach material from the Holderness coast is carried farther south to Lincolnshire and beyond.

Before we look at the Lincolnshire coast we must visit the south bank of the Humber near Barton. Here there is a raised bed of shingle running inland for some distance. The Humber may have deposited the pebbles when its estuary was wider and its bed higher. Leaving the Humber, we make our way down the Lincolnshire coast. It is flat but not depressing, as it has many sandy beaches, fringed by sand-dunes. The shingle, made up of the pebbles from the boulder clay and the material brought southward by beach drifting, is consistently interesting, but after we have progressed three miles south of Skegness and turned south-eastward to the Lincolnshire side of the Wash, our interest wanes, because there is no shingle until we reach the Norfolk side. On that side we find extensive beds of it opposite Snettisham. Longshore drifting has carried it into the Wash from the north Norfolk coast. This trend, you will note, is opposite to the general direction of drifting (north to south) along all the east coast of England. Somewhere near Sheringham the Norfolk beach material travels westward along the Norfolk coast and then southward into the Wash, but, east of Sheringham, the pebbles follow the general trend of east coast drifting and travel south-eastward down that coast. The reason for this exception to the general rule becomes clear when you look at a map of England. Norfolk bulges out into the North Sea. Its north coast runs roughly E.–W. The waves of the North Sea approaching from the north-east strike that coast obliquely and carry the shingle towards the Wash, but, beyond Sheringham, the coastline begins to turn southward and the waves then drive the beach material down the coast towards Suffolk. Changes of wind, and therefore of wave direction, produce other results, of course, but the dominant winds always prevail in the end and effect this exception to the general tendency of east coast pebbles to make their way southward.

The shape of Norfolk is also responsible for the slowing down of this movement of beach material. Another glance at the map will show why that is so. Its protrusion so far out into the North Sea makes it a gigantic barrier against the southward drift of pebbles down the coast. This accounts to some extent for the fine stretches of shingle on the north Norfolk beaches. Ultimately, of course, the pebbles west of Sheringham are forced round the corner and travel down to join the extensive shingle beds on the Suffolk coast.

A very shallow sea creeps in and out of the Wash and on the Norfolk beaches to the east of it, so the distance between high- and low-water marks is very great. Between them there are expanses of sand and mud. The waves that wash the shores of a shallow sea have very little transporting power when the tide is in, because they have broken far away from the shore. Beds of boulder clay, deposited by glaciers on the bed of the sea, are eroded by these distant breakers and their pebbles are carried along in a direction parallel to the beach. They form spits of shingle out beyond the flats of sand and silt. These 'offshore bars' are a conspicuous feature of this most interesting coast.

Making our way eastwards from the Wash, we come to Hunstanton, which lies at the edge of a large tract of chalk country extending nearly to Sheringham. The chalk outcrops impressively at Hunstanton in high and almost vertical cliffs. These are the last rock cliffs of any prominence that we shall see until we have made the long journey to the North Foreland in Kent. It must not be inferred from this statement that all that huge stretch of coast is dull, flat and uninteresting. On the contrary, much of it is exciting, especially to the pebble-collector.

The Hunstanton chalk is not uniformly white. The upper cliff consists of white chalk; beneath it is a stratum of red chalk about a yard thick, containing ammonites and other fossils; the base of the cliff is a layer of a variety of sandstone, known to geologists as carstone. It contains minute grains of iron ore of a dark brown colour. The sea abrades the bottom of the cliff, undercutting the white chalk and, from time to time, masses of the upper chalk cliff crash down to the beach. There the waves break up the blocks, releasing the hard flints. Pebbles of flint consequently make up a high proportion of the shingle.

Beyond the cliffs is a long line of sand-dunes bordered by shingle. This beach pattern goes on, with slight variation, to Brancaster and beyond. A good pebble beach separates Brancaster golf-course from the shore sand. A little farther along we come to the fascinating Scolt Head Island, one of the areas under the protection of the National Trust. Extending from Brancaster Harbour to Burnham Harbour, the island is four miles long. A shingle beach runs all the way along its northern side and from it broader ridges of shingle branch out southward towards the mainland. Marshes lie between these ridges. The island is a most striking example of the effects of the transportation of beach material by the tides. Experts who have investigated the movements of shingle on this part of the Norfolk coast have come to the conclusion that the island originated as an offshore bar. The constant drifting of shingle to the west lengthened it in that direction. From time to time, however, winds and waves from the north-west held up the westward prolongation and curved the tip of the shingle southward. Each of the southward-branching ridges was probably produced in this way. The island continues to grow ever westward as the dominant winds bring beach material to lengthen it in that direction. Almost all the pebbles in these beds of shingle are flint, derived from the white chalk that the sea has eroded.

Sand-dunes, marshes, shingle spits and offshore bars continue to be the characteristic of the coast as we go eastward. Spreads and ridges of shingle lie to the east of Wells Harbour and, as we approach Morston, we see more beds of shingle and a long bank of it above the level of the present beach. It is a raised beach and was probably formed before the end of the Ice Age. We are now very near to a huge stretch of shingle extending for miles, the longest pebble ridge on the Norfolk coast. This is Blakeney Point. Beginning at Weybourne it runs for 7½ miles westward to its tip, Far Point. As on Scolt Head Island, branching ridges of shingle run off here and there in a southerly direction, marking, as on the Island, the stages in the growth of the spit. The direction of drift is also westward. In fact, the similarities between Scolt Head Island and Blakeney Point afford some evidence that each of them originated in the same way, as an offshore bar, the former developing into an island, the latter into a spit.

The Blakeney Point pebbles are of flint from the local chalk, Norwich red crag from Sheringham and assorted material from the boulder clay scoured from the bed of the very shallow sea. Winter winds sometimes lash this sea to fury and it then makes breaches in the ridge. The most noteworthy effect of these storms is that the Blakeney Point pebbles show very little grading. They are mixed together, big and little, for most of the length of the ridge.

Returning now to Weybourne, we find ourselves at the beginning of another fine stretch of shingle that runs below the cliffs of boulder clay all the way to Sheringham. Flint pebbles are abundant, mixed with others of diverse origin eroded from the glacial deposit. As the boulder clay persists as far as Happisburgh, over 20 miles away, the beaches below the clay are fed from the soft cliffs with a never-ending supply of ice-borne pebbles that have travelled far and cannot fail to hold the interest and rouse the curiosity of the collector. The cliffs themselves are of special interest to the geologist, for certain sections of them unfold to him the history of the Ice Age deposits on the North Sea coast. They rise above the attractive beach of Sheringham about 100 feet. The Sheringham and Cromer beaches lie on a platform of chalk that the waves have cut down. This chalk is the source of enormous numbers of flint pebbles that abound on the beaches of these pleasant resorts and elsewhere on the north and north-eastern coast of Norfolk. Cromer is another Mecca for the pebble-collector. There are fossil-bearing flints and glacial pebbles galore, milky quartz and occasional agate, chalcedony and carnelian. Pieces of Whitby jet are sometimes found and, more rarely, amber. As we have now passed Sheringham, you must remember that we have got back into the region of the southward drifting of beach material. It goes on without further interruption all the way to Dover.

There is low coast from Happisburgh right down to Yarmouth, but it is certainly not dull. Its pattern resembles that of the coastline to the east of Blakeney Point in its dunes and its shingle ridges lying far out beyond high-water mark. The main difference is that the shingle is not broken up into offshore bars, but is continuous for a very long way. Boulder clay and southward drifting are the chief contributions to this shingle. At Yarmouth we have one of the outstanding examples of the effects of longshore drifting. In Yarmouth's earliest days its inhabitants had to wage long and costly battles against the accumulating pebbles washed down from the north and blocking up the mouths of the rivers Yare, Waveney and Bure. A long spit of sand and shingle ran down the coast from Caister, through which the fishermen of Yarmouth cut channels from time to time to give free passage to their boats. In the fourteenth century the spit had grown so far to the south that the river Yare could not reach the sea above a point only $2\frac{1}{2}$ miles north of Lowestoft. The Yarmouth people must have had more than enough of shingle, yet those of Lowestoft now wish for more. They need it to protect their exposed coast. Much of the shingle which would have drifted southwards from Yarmouth to Lowestoft is held and piled up behind the Gorleston piers. The coast from Gorleston to Aldeburgh, over 30 miles in all, bordered by soft cliffs of boulder clay, gravel and sand, has suffered severely from erosion. It has some fine shingle beaches. Here again there was a surfeit of shingle. Little harbours that were in existence in the fourteenth century have ceased to exist, having long ago been blocked up with shingle after repeated efforts to cut channels through the ridges. Covehithe Ness is the most impressive of the pebble accumulations on this piece of coast, but the pebbles of all the Norfolk and Suffolk beaches are interesting, as indeed they are on most of the east coast.

Proceeding beyond Aldeburgh, we come to the greatest expanse of shingle on all that coast, Orford Ness. As this was described in

110

Chapter I, we can pass quickly on to Felixstowe and the estuary of the Orwell. Pebbles from Orford Ness drift down that coast and form a spit across the mouth of the river Deben. Southward drifting has created a much bigger mass of shingle at the mouth of the Orwell. It is the promontory called Landguard Point, jutting out to the south beyond Felixstowe. The beach of that resort is of never-failing attraction to the pebble-hunter. Among the innumerable pebbles of flint are many of quartz and some of jet that has drifted down from Whitby, chalcedony, agate, carnelian and jasper. You may even be lucky enough to find a piece of amber. Also there are chocolate-coloured pebbles which are peculiar to the Suffolk coast and therefore deserve some explanation of their origin. They were derived from the London clay, which, together with red crag, is the cliff material from Harwich to Frinton. The name 'London clay' is given to that expansive layer of clay that not only lies below the metropolis but extends beyond it for many miles. 'Red Crag' is a deposit laid down before the Ice Age. It consists of reddish-brown shelly sand derived from old banks of sand and shells.

The London clay lies below the crag and runs out beneath the shallow sea. During the ages that have elapsed since this coast was formed the sea-water has effected some chemical change in the clay. The chocolate stones, scoured by the sea out of its bed, are the products of this change. It was found that these stones possessed the properties of a natural cement. Known locally as cement-stones, they were dredged up from the sea-bottom, taken to mills in Harwich and ground into cement.

Another curious feature of this stretch of the Suffolk coast is a layer, below the red crag, of fossil bones and teeth of sharks and other creatures, mixed up with lumps or pebbles from the London clay. Bones contain a high percentage of phosphate of lime, which, as everyone knows, is excellent manure. A great Cambridge mineralogist of the early nineteenth century discovered that all these lumps had become so imbued with phosphate that they were likely to be of the greatest use to farmers. Hundreds of tons of the

111

phosphatic nodules were carted away from the Suffolk beaches to mills in London, there to be ground to powder and sold to farmers as manure. They have a smooth surface, the soft clay having been hardened by the phosphate of lime, and they are reddish-brown in colour. The local name for them for many years was 'coprolites', because it was erroneously thought that they were the fossilized droppings of the creatures whose bones were deposited in the Suffolk bone-bed (Greek: Kopros = dung).

There are some good and varied beds of shingle at the Naze and between Frinton and Clacton. The St. Osyth marshes are bordered by a broad stretch of pebbles, but this is the last section of the east coast to appeal to the collector until we get beyond the mouth of the Thames. Mud-flats, saltings and marsh creeks are the main feature of the south Essex coast.

The Kentish side of the estuary, bounded by London clay, is also marshy until we pass the Isle of Sheppey, and it remains flat and dull to Seasalter. Then the London clay rises out of the mud. Cliffs of it run almost all the way to Reculver, where, at last, we come upon a sandy beach extending nearly to Birchington. We have now reached the Isle of Thanet, a chalk 'island', which was separated from the rest of north-east Kent by a strait almost 2 miles wide until the sixteenth century, when the strait dried up, leaving a broad belt of alluvium from the Reculver area on the north coast to Pegwell Bay on the east. The rivers Wantsum and Stour now lie roughly in the former channel. The chalk of the Isle of Thanet comes out on the north coast in a line of fine sheer cliffs, of which the eastern extremity is the North Foreland, where the cliffs turn southward to Ramsgate. There they end and give place to the broad sands of Pegwell Bay and Sandwich Bay, which lie at the eastern entrance of the former strait. Behind them the river Stour runs through the belt of alluvium.

It is here, in Sandwich Bay, that we find two extensive and interesting beds of shingle. One of them runs from Ebbsfleet to Stonar. If we ignore a break in it at Richborough, it is about 3 miles long. The river Stour encloses it in a loop which narrows down to a very small opening at Richborough. Nearly all the pebbles are of flint. They have drifted down from the chalk of the Isle of Thanet. The other bed is nearer the sea. Beginning at Deal, it runs up the coast for $3\frac{1}{2}$ miles in the form of a spit. Its pebbles are also of flint, but they are derived, not from the Isle of Thanet chalk by southward drifting, but from the chalk south of Deal by northward drifting. Consequently, the pebbles of these two beds have been accumulated by drift in two precisely opposite directions, an anomaly which has yet to be explained.

The pebble beaches of Sandwich and Deal are well worth exploration. Among the many flints there are pebbles of quartz and its chalcedonic varieties. Some excellent specimens of carnelian and sard have been found there. Coming round the corner of the South Foreland from Walmer, we see the high, white cliffs of Dover rising vertically from the beaches. The chalk continues nearly to Folkstone, contributing thousands of flint nodules to the shore. They help to some extent to slow down the erosion.

(B) THE SOUTH COAST: DOVER TO LAND'S END

Now that we have turned the corner into the English Channel, we must keep in mind all the way to Land's End that the trend of longshore drifting is up the Channel, that is from west to east, and that on nearly every shingle beach we shall find pebbles that have travelled there from more westerly beaches. Much of the shingle at Hythe and Dymchurch has drifted up from the vast spread at Dungeness. Having already looked in Chapter I at that great shingle foreland, we can hurry on past Rye and Winchelsea and the shingle which even now adds to the Dungeness accumulation by eastward drifting.

So we come to Fairlight from the flat coast of Romney Marsh, to find a line of cliffs running westward through Hastings to Bexhill. They are composed of clay and sandstone. The latter is fine-grained and of a pale yellow colour. Many pebbles formed from this rock are to be found on the Bexhill, Hastings and Fairlight beaches, mingling with abundant flints and brown, red and grey quartzite, shale, chert and grit. At the Pevensey Levels, beyond Bexhill, we come upon the eastern end of the great shingle bed that runs here all the way from Eastbourne. Known generally as the Crumbles, sometimes as Langley Point, it is a pebble beach vast enough to satisfy the most voracious of pebble-seekers. Some of the fulls are over a mile long. The chalk of the Beachy Head cliffs has contributed flint pebbles galore to the Crumbles. A belt of greensand country comes down to the sea between Eastbourne and Pevensey and from it have come numerous pebbles of chert. Eastward drifting has brought to this beach some far travellers from the south-western coast to relieve the monotony of the endless flint and chert. Pebbles of granite, grit, quartz, quartzite of several colours and a few pieces of agate, carnelian and other translucent stones reveal themselves to the discerning searcher.

Eastbourne beach also has plentiful and interesting shingle, which is impeded to some extent from drifting eastward by groynes. Beachy Head also helps to slow down the movement of beach material as it acts as a huge, natural groyne. This magnificent headland is the point at which the South Downs meet the sea. Its vertical cliffs, 500 feet high, of white chalk are a most impressive introduction to the chalk coast of Sussex. The cliffs go on with very little interruption through Seaford, Newhaven, Brighton, Shoreham, Worthing and Littlehampton, almost to Bognor Regis, where the chalk country ends. There are shingle beaches of good quality for most of the way. Naturally, the most prevalent pebbles are of flint, but longshore drifting has added to them many and varied pebbles from more westerly beaches. The most striking sections of coastline are between Beachy Head and Cuckmere Haven, where the clean, white chalk of the Seven Sisters rises almost vertically, and between Rottingdean and Brighton, where a sea-wall protects the fine, chalk cliffs from erosion. The spit of shingle at the mouth of the river Cuckmere deserves to be visited. Here and at many other parts of the Sussex chalk coast we can see the effects of erosion upon the cliffs, for the sea washes over a chalk platform from which the now vanished cliffs formerly rose. Those cliffs stood much farther out to sea. The material of which they were made has produced inexhaustible supplies of shingle. Yet even that quantity is insignificant in comparison with the huge mass of land that formerly connected Britain with France. That great isthmus consisted almost wholly of chalk. It disappeared in comparatively recent geological times, possibly at the end of the Ice Age, some 10,000 years ago. The chalk that now lies beneath the Straits of Dover has yielded an incalculable amount of flint pebbles to the beaches of our southeast coast.

To all its visitors except the most zealous of pebble-collectors Brighton beach seems to have far too much shingle and also too much of the same kind. Yet, over a century ago, it was one of the haunts of those who took up the then fashionable pursuit of collecting pebbles for the display cabinet. They collected and laboriously hammered flint pebbles in the hope of finding an internal surface that revealed fossilized remains in a pleasingly intricate pattern. These they would take to the local lapidaries for cutting and polishing. Of the thousands who now throng the Brighton beach, how many are thus engaged? Perhaps none, but there are still many fossiliferous flints there and many a flint pebble would repay the cost of its fashioning in the pleasure it gives to the beholder.

Shingle abounds between Shoreham and Worthing. The eastward drifting of it has turned the mouth of the river Adur more than a mile to the east. It was a constant menace to Shoreham Harbour until the building of the protected opening to the harbour in the last century prevented further blockages. Much of the great shingle beds at Lancing and Shoreham now lies above the high-water mark of ordinary tides, but storms hurl it inland and thus broaden the pebble bed. There is somewhat less shingle as we go west of Worthing towards Littlehampton. We are now passing out of the region of chalk cliffs and making our way along a comparatively low coast to Bognor Regis, where the chalk gives way to London clay, sandstone and sandy limestone. Pebbles from the neighbouring Selsey Bill and from the Isle of Wight drift eastward along this stretch of coast.

Selsey Bill has much the same shape as Dungeness. It is in every respect a 'ness', but it lacks the huge expanse of shingle that has accumulated to form the latter. Formerly an island, it is still virtually so, because a low-lying marsh running from Bracklesham Bay to Pagham Harbour almost separates it from the mainland. The Bill and the foreshores on each side of it consist of a soft sandstone known to geologists as the Bracklesham Beds. Selsey and Bracklesham Bay are famous for the large range of marine fossils that are found in these beds. On both coasts of the Bill there is good and varied shingle, much of which is derived from drifting from the beaches of Hampshire, the Isle of Wight and farther west. The shingle on the western side of the Bill is unstable. If gales blowing up the Channel coincide with high tides they wash away many of the pebbles.

We now reach a complicated section of coast, heavily indented and geologically varied. This is the stretch from Chichester Harbour to the western entrance to the Solent, with the Isle of Wight lying to the south. The simplest plan will be to take first the mainland coast, as it demands much less attention than the more attractive beaches of the Isle of Wight. In each case it is essential to remember that the direction of longshore drifting is eastward.

Alluvium and mud-flats characterize much of the mainland coast. Apart from the chalk of the Appledram, Emsworth and Havant coast, and of the northern parts of Thorney, Hayling and Portsea Islands, clay, sand and gravel soils constitute the mainland. Shingle beaches, consisting mainly of pebbles of hard chalk and flint, line this coast but not continuously. There is a long strip of shingle at Portsmouth Harbour and a very broad and deep one on the south-western corner of Hayling Island.

The relative hardness of the Isle of Wight rocks has determined the lozenge shape of that island. A high ridge of chalk runs across the island from the Needles in the west to the gloriously white Culver Cliff in the east. Limestone, marl, sandstone and clay make up the ground to the north of the chalk ridge. To the south there are sandstone, limestone, shale, marl and clay, but in the south-east the chalk rises again to form the highest part of the island. There is such similarity between the rocks in the north of the island and those on the Hampshire side of the Solent on the one hand, and between the rocks of the rest of the island and those of the Swanage district on the other, that the former union of the island with the mainland can be easily understood. Land once lay between the Isle of Wight and Hampshire, Bournemouth Bay and the Isle of Purbeck.

The chalk out of which the Needles have been cut is very hard, much harder than the white cliffs we have already observed at so many places on this tour of the coast. Since they were deposited they have lain undisturbed but the chalk of the Needles and the adjacent ridge was folded over by earth movements under great pressure. It was this pressure that hardened the Isle of Wight chalk. It accounts for the projection of the ridge into the sea at the western extremity of the island. The waves have more easily eroded the softer rocks lying to the north and south of the Needles. Thus the island has acquired its shape.

The pebble beaches of the Isle of Wight are a rich deposit of stones that gladden the collector. In addition to the predominating flint, limestone and sandstone derived from the island's rocks, there is a most gratifying variety of other pebbles. From Culver Cliff through Sandown and Shanklin to Luccombe there is excellent shingle. The beaches of Bonchurch, Ventnor and Niton are equally satisfying. The quartz family is well represented from pure quartz or rock crystal to jasper. Agate and carnelian can also be found. Sandown Bay is peculiarly rich in fossil-bearing flint pebbles. Many of them contain fossil sponges with beautifully delicate spicula.

Before we proceed further to the west we must glance at a shingle spit of no little interest on the mainland. This is the Hurst Castle spit between Christchurch Bay and the Solent. It runs out to sea in a south-easterly direction for over a mile, then turns to the east for about half a mile, throwing out lateral ridges to the N.N.W. The first of these three sections demonstrates the eastward drifting of beach material, the second shows that the spit had reached deep water and must take a left-hand turn to continue its growth, and the lateral ridges show the effect of northeast winds blowing down the Solent and causing the spit to bend backwards.

The spit is a continuation of the long bed of shingle on Milford beach. From this beach cliffs of sand and clay line the long sweep of Christchurch Bay for some miles and their erosion brings down material to the foreshore. From observations of the movement of this material it has been concluded that strong south-east winds drive more of it westward than is driven eastward by south-west winds. Consequently, this part of Christchurch Bay furnishes an exception to the general tendency of drift along the south coast. On the other hand, a long spit of sand and shingle runs back from Hengistbury Head at the western end of the bay for over 2 miles though only the first $\frac{3}{4}$ mile is stable. Much of this shingle, including very large pebbles of flint, has travelled eastward round Hengistbury Head from Bournemouth Bay.

The coast of that bay is of clay and sandstone and its shingle is similar to that of Christchurch Bay. Poole Harbour and Studland Bay have attractive dunes, saltings and sandbanks, but little shingle of interest. We have now reached the Isle of Purbeck, which has a coast of great beauty and variety. In its alternating hard and soft rocks it clearly shows how the former resist erosion and how the latter yield to it. The technical term for this is 'differential erosion', and we shall have occasion to notice it when we survey the west coast.

The first of the hard promontories that we see is Ballard Point, with the Old Harry rocks and the Foreland. The vertical cliffs of hard, white chalk are part of the same chalk ridge that traverses the Isle of Wight. To the south of the chalk is a broad belt of clay, which the sea has cut back to form the lovely Swanage Bay. Then come hard rocks again. They are of Purbeck limestone, a hard, compact stone widely used in the decoration of important buildings. The pebbles formed from it respond well to polishing. Turning to the west round Durlston Point, we see a long line of high vertical cliffs, with Portland stone in the lower, and Purbeck stone in the upper, part. Portland stone is another hard limestone in much use for building. It contains many fossils. In these cliffs are nodules of chert.

As soon as we pass St. Alban's Head, we find the coast cut back, because the hard rocks have been underlain by clay, with some layers of shale and limestone running through it. This clay, of a very dark grey colour, is known as Kimmeridge clay, taking its name from Kimmeridge Bay on this piece of coast. It appears in many other parts of England.

In the next 5 miles is to be found some of the most delightful coast scenery in England, from Worbarrow Bay, past Mupe Bay, Lulworth Cove, Stair Hole and Durdle Door to Bat's Head. The hard rocks are Portland and Purbeck limestone and chalk. At Worbarrow Bay and Lulworth Cove the sea has broken through the outer defences of Portland stone and, having eaten away the layer of clay behind, is now trying to erode the chalk, which forms the inner defences. In these and other bays on the south side of the Isle of Purbeck, the pebbles are graded in an unusual manner, the larger being in the centre of the bay, the smaller at the sides. Most of the pebbles are of hard chalk, flint, chert, Purbeck limestone, Portland limestone, and sandstone, with an admixture of varieties from the beaches of Weymouth, Devon and Cornwall.

From the Isle of Purbeck to the Isle of Portland we have the coast of Weymouth Bay. It is a geological inter-mixture of chalk, gault, greensand, clay, grit and Purbeck and Portland limestones, so the shingle of the beaches is well varied. Two large belts of shingle must be specially mentioned. One of them runs down the west side of Weymouth Bay for about 2 miles. The pebbles decrease in size as the shingle approaches Weymouth beach, which consists mostly of sand. Flint pebbles predominate in this belt. The other is Portland beach. It runs up from Portland towards

Weymouth for $1\frac{1}{2}$ miles and has been formed of pebbles derived from the two limestones, Purbeck and Portland, of the Isle. The building of Portland breakwater has retarded the growth of this beach. Although it is in contact with Chesil Beach at one part, it is geologically quite distinct from it.

As Chapter I contained a description of the famous Chesil Beach, we can pass on to the beaches of the widely sweeping Lyme Bay. From Bridport (which, you may recall, is the western end of Chesil Beach) to Sidmouth and beyond the rocks of Lyme Bay are of many kinds. In their variety they produce coast scenery of no little charm. Blue and yellow cliffs of shale and limestone face the beaches for some miles around Charmouth and Lyme Regis; those of Seaton and Sidmouth consist of red marl, and those of Budleigh Salterton are of dark red sandstone, but here and there we find chalk, chert, shale, greensand and clay. On the cliffs between the mouth of the Axe and Lyme Regis the strata of chalk, clay and greensand lie upon the limestones, shales and marls at an angle which sometimes slopes towards the sea. If the sea undercuts the cliffs at those points the upper strata may slide over the lower and plunge downwards. There have been some spectacular landslides of this kind. One at Axmouth in 1839 produced the collapse of eight million tons of earth. Great mounds of it lay on the beach and a huge ridge of greensand suddenly rose out of the sea. Erosion has since disposed of the ridge and the mounds, adding copious material to the shingle of the Lyme Bay beaches.

The pebbles of these beaches are mostly flint and chert, but there is much limestone, sandstone and shale. The biggest spreads of shingle are the spit which turns the mouth of the Char to the east and the long belt that runs with little interruption from Branscombe for some miles towards Sidmouth.

On the other side of the river Otter are the cliffs of Budleigh Salterton. They are of dark red sandstone. In these cliffs there lie exposed the extraordinary pebble-beds which all pebble-collectors should strive to visit, for from this deposit pebbles of unusual interest have travelled eastward to most of the beaches on the whole of the south coast of England. They are all well rounded, having been transported to Budleigh Salterton, it is believed, many millions of years ago by turbulent water that poured from the west over land now beneath the sea. Most of the pebbles are of dark brown quartzite and grit.

Soon after passing Budleigh Salterton we enter upon a red coast, the rocks of which are formed of sandstone, clay, marl and breccia. These formations continue all the way to Babbacombe, near Torquay. The word 'breccia' is of Italian origin and means the rubbish of broken walls. Breccia is formed when a mass of rock is fractured by the great pressure of earth-movements and the rock is crushed into small angular fragments. These fragments become consolidated by a process of natural cementation. Consequently, a breccia resembles a conglomerate, but in the former the fragments are angular and in the latter they are rounded. Pebbles of breccia are very attractive, especially when cut and polished. The shingle of this coast yields some good specimens of them, among many of red sandstone. Langstone Point on the western side of the Exe estuary is formed of breccia and bands of it appear in the cliffs for most of the way to Dawlish.

There is good shingle in the Teignmouth district. The bar of shingle and sand at the mouth of the river Teign, running to the north-east from the Ness, fluctuates in size and in shape according to the severity of tides and winds.

As we proceed southward along the Devon coast we come to a region of much older and more diverse rocks. Hitherto we have encountered few rocks that were not of sedimentary origin, but now in Devon and Cornwall we shall come upon many that are igneous and some that are metamorphic. The formations are of great complexity and the scenery is therefore most pleasantly varied. Limestone, slate, sandstone, shale, grit and dolerite make up the rocks of Torquay and Torbay. The pebbles formed from these rocks predominate in the shingle of the beaches. There are good ridges of shingle on Oddicombe and Babbacombe beaches. Of the two Torquay promontories, Black Head is a tough mass of dolerite, and Hope's Nose is of limestone. Going south through Paignton we pass along a coast of red sandstone, but near Broad Sands and its pebble ridge we enter a limestone area. The Brixham cliffs are of limestone and so is Berry Head, the promontory at the southern end of Tor Bay.

On the other side of Berry Head we come to Start Bay, a wide sweep, on which the pebble-hunter will find much to occupy himself, for, between the estuary of the Dart and Start Point, a distance of some 10 miles, there is a series of shingle beaches of exceptional interest. The pebbles are well rounded and are derived from the diverse rocks that line this lovely coast: sandstone, grit, shale, green schist, quartzite, slate, red slate and dolerite. There are also pebbles of granite, brought down to the beach by the river Dart from the granite mass of Dartmoor.

In the middle of Start Bay is a bed of shingle that must not be missed. This is the extensive bar at Torcross that encloses the lagoon called Slapton Ley. There is one very unusual feature about it. Its pebbles do not come from the rocks of the Bay. Many of them are flints, yet there is no chalk or other flint-bearing rock near to Torcross. The other pebbles are quartz, including very small ones that are pear-shaped, and granite from Dartmoor. A smaller but very pleasant shingle beach that is somewhat similar is at Blackpool (as unlike its Lancastrian namesake as any part of the coast of the British Isles could be), between Slapton and the Dart estuary. Another good belt of shingle lies above Bee Sands, between Slapton and Start Point.

Start Point, Prawle Point, Bolt Head and Bolt Tail form the southern tip of Devonshire. These rugged promontories are made of metamorphic rocks of extreme age, green schist and mica schist veined with quartz. A freshly broken piece of mica schist has a beautiful lustre.

From Bolt Tail to Plymouth the coast continues to be impressive. It has headlands of hard sandstone with occasional dolerite. There are no great expanses of shingle, but its pebbles, many of which have drifted from the Cornish beaches, are of unfailing interest. Plymouth's pretty cliffs are composed of limestone, containing many unusual fossil corals, of types only found here and at Torquay.

The enchanting coast of the Cornish peninsula now lies ahead of us. From Plymouth Sound to Mevagissey most of the cliffs are formed of slate and grit. They are mainly grey in colour, but there are variations from green to red. The slate varies also in its texture and durability. Some of it is hard and glossy, but some of it approximates to shale of a muddy kind. Pebbles of this rock are not very attractive, but many of them have veins of quartz and these look well when polished. There are few shingle beaches of any extent east of Mevagissey. Igneous rocks, mostly of dolerite, are to be seen in the headland beyond Par. The shingle becomes more frequent, but in small beaches, between Veryan Bay and the Lizard; all of it is good and is a representative assortment of the diversified rock structures.

The Lizard peninsula is unique in the rich colouring of its cliffs and in the nature and formation of its rocks. These are so complex that only a geological map of large scale can show them clearly and in detail. Briefly, the predominant rock is serpentine, both green and mottled red. It gives the Lizard cliffs their glorious colours from Cadgwith nearly to the Lizard Point, which is a mass of schist, and right round for most of the way from Kynance Cove to Mullion. Innumerable dykes of gabbro run through the serpentine and come out on the face of the cliffs. Gneiss, in beautiful foliations, is seen to best advantage in the Man o' War Rocks, bands of quartzite and dykes of granite run through much of the schist, and pebbles of granite travel down the coast from St. Michael's Mount and Trewavas Head. The pebbles formed from both the green and the yellow serpentine, the gneiss and the schist are particularly pleasing. One of the local industries is the cutting, fashioning and polishing of serpentine, but the serious pebble-collector must not be so absorbed in that fascinating rock as to forget the others that the Lizard provides.

As we continue up the coast towards Mount's Bay we cross

123

several attractive and rewarding beaches. Then, between Baulk Head and Porthleven Harbour is a straight sandy beach for $2\frac{1}{2}$ miles. An extraordinary spread of shingle lies just beyond the middle of this stretch. It is Loe Bar. It encloses the lovely fresh-water lake called Loe Pool. The spread is over 400 yards long and 200 yards wide. This is small in comparison with most of the expansions of shingle that we have examined, but it has a peculiar quality. Most of the pebbles are of flint, despite the fact that no flint-bearing strata are to be found in western Cornwall, though there is some in the Scilly Isles. The same peculiarity is to be seen at Prah Sands, about 4 miles farther along. It has puzzled geologists for a long time. It may be that the flints came from rocks which have long ago disappeared as the result of denudation.

The coast from Porthleven to Newlyn is of slate, granite and greenstone. The pebble-collector should linger on the Marazion and Penzance beaches as long as possible, for here he should find many choice specimens for his cabinet. Pebbles of granite, some of them porphyritic, quartz, quartzite, quartz-veined slate, greenstone, serpentine, jasper in various shades, agate, chalcedony, citrine, carnelian and amethystine quartz, together with fossiliferous flints await his discerning scrutiny. The pebbles of these and neighbouring beaches on the Cornish coast are remarkable, not only for their lustrous beauty when cut and polished, but also for the extent of their geological range.

From Mousehole, round Land's End to Cape Cornwall, the cliffs are all of granite. They are the edge of the huge mass of granite that forms the western knob of the Cornish peninsula and they present a sturdy front against the fierce Atlantic gales. Their castellated form almost suggests that they have been established there for that very purpose.

(C) THE WEST COAST: LAND'S END TO THE SOLWAY FIRTH

The long coast we are now about to explore is both deeply and widely indented, as much of it is washed by waves of long 'fetch'. The dominant wind is from the south-west, so the direction of longshore drifting is northward. When the coast runs from west to east, e.g. North Wales, the trend will naturally be eastward.

The massive granite cliffs from Land's End to Cape Cornwall contribute pebbles of that rock to the beach of Whitesand Bay. The beach at Cape Cornwall is very limited but it contains a very satisfactory assortment of pebbles. Although granite is the main rock in the cliffs all the way to St. Ives Bay, the greyness is relieved here and there by greenstone, especially between Cape Cornwall and Pendeen Watch. At Porthmeor Cove, one of the many delightful coves on that coast, the rocks are of granite, greenstone and slate. The two biggest promontories, Gurnard's Head and St. Ives Head, consist of greenstone.

At St. Ives we leave the granite region for a low coast of sandstone, grit and slate. From Carbis Bay to Godrevy Point there are 5 miles of sandy beach, most of which is backed by dunes. There is comparatively little shingle, but it is well worth inspection. The dune coast is succeeded by imposing and rugged cliffs of sandstone and slate continuing for at least 10 miles between Navax Point and St. Agnes Head. At first there is little, if any, beach at the cliff foot, but some shingle lies below the long line of cliffs that edge Reskajeage Downs and at Portreath and Porth Towan. The pebbles, like those of all the Cornish beaches, are not merely those that have been formed from the local rocks. Sandy shale and slate continue for some miles, though interrupted by the granite of Cligga Head. The Newquay cliffs are of hard, black shale. Perran Beach is a huge expanse of sand, backed by very high dunes. This and the fine beaches of Crantock, Fistral Bay, Newquay Bay, the great sweep of Watergate Bay, Beacon Cove and Mawgan Porth, are of fine, shelly sand with little but very varied and interesting shingle.

Some little distance north of Mawgan Porth, and near Bedruthan Steps, we come upon cliffs of sandstone and shale, which go on to Port Isaac, but here and there are outcrops of tough, volcanic rock. This rock forms the headlands, of which the most prominent are Park Head, Trevose Head and Pentire Point. The lava of which Pentire Point is formed is famous for its curious appearance. It resembles a heap of pillows. The rock, known as 'pillow lava', was probably erupted in a molten state from the sea-bed.

On this part of the Cornish coast there are raised beaches, usually elevated about 10 feet. One of the best of these is at Tre-betherick Point, near Padstow. The river Camel comes out into Padstow Bay in a wide estuary. It brings down to the coast vast quantities of fine sand. The bar in the bay consists of sand. Geologically interesting as this coast is, its shingle is scanty. We must make our way some distance to the north before the beds become at all extensive. A coast of slate and shale cliffs, with headlands of greenstone, goes on for most of the way to Tintagel. The lovely Trebarwith Strand and Hole Beach are backed by lava, then comes slate again, to be followed by formations of great complexity at Tintagel, where violent earth-movements have caused much thrusting and crumpling.

The igneous rocks disappear at Boscastle, and then come cliffs of shale, sandstone and chert. In fact, the whole stretch of coast from Boscastle to Appledore in Barnstaple Bay may be said to consist of dark shale, sandstone and occasional limestone and chert. There is not much shingle on the sandy beaches of Wide-mouth Bay and Bude. Fragments from the cliffs are more quickly ground by the crushing power of the long Atlantic rollers on this exposed coast than on the more sheltered beaches east of Hartland Point. At that corner, where the coast running north from Bude turns sharply east towards Clovelly, is some of the most impressive cliff scenery in England. The Hartland rocks are of shale and sandstone. A beach of boulders and very large pebbles, mainly derived from these rocks, lies below the cliffs for most of the way from Hartland Point to Clovelly, but only the agile and strenuous pebble-collectors can make their way down to it. Another beach of boulders and large pebbles lies below the cliffs between Pepper-combe and Westward Ho! but the first shingle bed of any great size comes into view at Westward Ho! The rivers Taw and Torridge meet in one estuary to the north of the ridge. The shingle ridge, over a mile long, is a massive accumulation of very large ovoid pebbles and boulders. Most of them are too big to have been carried down by the two rivers. Only longshore drifting from the south-west can account for the accumulation.

There are no cliffs here, but an enormous range of sand-dunes extends from Westward Ho! to Croyde Bay. Baggy Point with its high sandstone cliffs juts out straight, and far to the east, thus hindering the transportation of pebbles from the south. Here again, and at Saunton, where there is some good shingle, the raised beach can be seen. There is regular alternation of slate and sandstone rocks for the next 25 miles. The sandstone of Baggy Point and Morte Bay is succeeded by the slates of Morte Point, Bull Point, Lee, Ilfracombe and Combe Martin Bay. Then comes the sandstone of Trentishoe and Heddon's Mouth, the slate of Woody Bay, Lee Bay and Lynton, and the sandstone again of Foreland Point and on into Porlock Bay. Shingle, formed mainly from the local rocks, appears in most of the coves. The slates of Morte Point come out in sharp ridges on the lower part of the beach. They are glossy and have veins of quartz running through them. The blue-grey slates and shales of the Ilfracombe coast are also attractive, having a silvery sheen. Shingle, including boulders and large pebbles, lies along the beach of Porlock Bay, and at Porlock the eastward drifting has piled up a small cape of shingle around the harbour. It has also caused a large accumulation at Greenaleigh.

We are now approaching an area of softer rocks: marl, clay, impure limestone and soft shale, beginning near Minehead and going on along the southern shore of Bridgwater Bay to the estuary of the river Parret. These shores are much less exposed to the attack of the Atlantic breakers than those of Cornwall and North Devon and some of them enjoy the additional protection of storm beaches of piled-up shingle. The fine sand and alluvium between Minehead and Blue Anchor lies behind a belt of shingle. The eastward drifting of beach material has formed a large bar of shingle at the mouth of the Parret and has bent back the outlet of the river. It has also added ridges of shingle to Stert Point. There is very little shingle in Weston Bay and only a thin belt of it in Sand Bay. Harder and older rocks have now come into view. The Brean headland is of hard limestone. Massive limestone and old red sandstone are to be seen in the coast rocks between Clevedon and Portishead. The old red sandstone contains many agates. They may be found occasionally among the pebbles.

But we have now reached the Severn estuary, with its low, flat shores, muddy water, deposits of alluvium, and salt marshes. We must cross the estuary to the more open sea beaches of South Wales. As they run roughly east–west the longshore drift will be eastward, until we reach that point in Pembrokeshire where the coastline begins to turn northward again.

Avoiding the alluvium of the Usk estuary and the dock area of Cardiff, we can begin at Penarth Head. This Glamorganshire coast is formed of comparatively soft rocks, of no great height but of no little charm. The vertical cliffs appear to be painted in bands of colour. There are red and green marls, yellow and blue limestones and black shales. A wave-cut platform lies below them, cut from the same rocks. Limestone predominates as we go farther west towards Porthcawl. There are almost continuous cliffs of it all the way to Barry. Below the cliffs are pebble or boulder beaches, formed mostly from the cliff material. There is a large spread of shingle at Aberthaw containing many pebbles from the west. Rocks, mainly of limestone, go on a little way past Porthcawl, giving place to marl and then millstone grit before the shale of Swansea Bay begins at Port Talbot.

At the western end of Swansea Bay we come to the Gower Peninsula, which, in its geological structure and coastal beauty, is of almost unique interest, situated though it is in juxtaposition to a highly industrialized area. The peninsula is a level plateau of limestone, which has been folded by earth-movements. They have also caused thrusts and faults in the strata in many places. There is a considerable amount of old red sandstone, especially at

Rhossili Bay, and of shale, notably in Port Eynon, Oxwich Bay, Oystermouth and bordering Llanrhidian Sands. From Mumbles Head, that juts out into Swansea Bay, cliffs of grey limestone form the south coast of the peninsula almost all the way to its western extremity, Worms Head. Very pleasant bays indent these cliffs at intervals, usually where faults in the strata have aided the attacks of the waves. A wave-cut platform lies below the limestone cliffs. Where there is shingle, most of the pebbles have originated from the limestone, sandstone and shale of the peninsula, the shape of which greatly impedes the drifting of beach material from the west. A glance at the map will make this clear at once. The peninsula runs out due west from the mainland, which is separated from it on its north side by the wide and long Burry Inlet going due east for 8 miles.

A large pebble ridge has developed at the seaward end of Burry Inlet into Whiteford Spit. Most of the pebbles are of limestone and have been transported up the western coast of the peninsula by wave-action, though a great authority has suggested that the source of these pebbles may have been a moraine that has long ago disappeared. A moraine consists of the debris left by a glacier after it has melted. This must remind us that we have now travelled far enough to the north to be back in that part of the country which bears evidence of the Ice Age. Ever since we left the Essex shores we have moved along the coasts of the un-glaciated part of England. Henceforward we shall have to make frequent reference to boulder clay, glacial drift and so forth.

One other interesting feature of Gower is its raised beaches. They can be seen on many parts of the coast on a kind of platform lying between the top edge of the cliffs and the present-day beach.

Returning to the mainland on the other side of Burry Inlet we find a coast of sand-dunes and marsh reaching to the famous sands of Pendine in Carmarthen Bay. After passing the joint estuary of the rivers Towy and Taf, however, we see a series of beaches of very large pebbles and boulders, mostly of limestone and sandstone that have drifted eastward from Pembrokeshire.

We are now about to explore the shores of that county which, to the pebble-seeker, are among the most fascinating in the British Isles. The western coast of Carmarthen Bay, north of Tenby, is mainly of shale, with some sandstone. At Saundersfoot is a shingle beach which has diminished in depth and extent in the last sixty years as the result of the eastward drifting of beach material. In the nineteenth century ships called at Saundersfoot for cargoes of coal. They dumped their ballast on the beach before they took the coal aboard. In course of time a large beach of ballast accumulated, consisting of stones from various parts of the British Isles and elsewhere. When Saundersfoot ceased to export coal, the piles of ballast not only ceased to grow but dwindled, as their material drifted away to the east. The pebble-collector must always have in mind the possibility that a stone on any part of our coast may have travelled there from a heap of ballast, for Saundersfoot is not the only place on the British coastline where ballast-dumping has gone on. One can seldom be absolutely certain of the original source of any pebble.

The very pleasant and largely unspoilt resort of Tenby is at the eastern end of a long series of magnificent limestone cliffs. Between Tenby and Giltar Point, to the south of it, is a fine sandy beach backed, first, by a storm beach of pebbles, and then by extensive sand dunes. The bulk of the shingle comes from the local rocks, limestone, sandstone and shale. The remainder are pebbles of various kinds scoured by the sea from boulder clay and stones from the raised beach at Giltar Point. Some ballast pebbles are also present.

The cliffs between Tenby and Angle are very like those of Gower peninsula in formation and colouring. They consist of grey limestone and, near Angle, old red sandstone, a pleasing contrast. The red rocks are especially striking in Manorbier Bay, Freshwater Bay East and Freshwater Bay West. Good and well-varied shingle lies in many of the delightful bays between Tenby and Milford Haven. Both the northern and the southern shores of the Haven are of the old red sandstone. At St. Ann's Head we are at the beginning of a coast that is scarcely equalled for beauty, diversity of colouring, stacks, arches and islands in all England and Wales. Vertical cliffs of limestone continue to Broad Haven in St. Bride's Bay. The rocks of that magnificent sweep possess wide variations of age, hardness and colour. Volcanic rocks are interspersed among sandstone, quartzite, limestone and shale and the cliff colours are black, grey, yellow and purple. Musselwick Bay displays the striking contrast of black shales and old red sandstone. As we go northwards along the shores of St. Bride's Bay we find the harder sandstone forming the headlands and the softer shale cut back into little bays: another example of differential erosion. The pebbles of the bays have originated for the most part from these rocks, but they are mingled with others of many kinds from the boulder clay. Near the northern end of the bay is the superb beach of Newgale, its fine expanse of sand fringed by a storm beach of rounded sandstone pebbles, many of which have travelled eastward along the northern shore.

The north Pembrokeshire coast from Newgale to Fishguard is even more impressive in its rock structure, the boldness of its headlands and the colouring of its cliffs. This great arm of land protruding westward above St. Bride's Bay is built of rocks that were laid down in the remotest geological ages: the Ordovician, a period of intense volcanic activity that began about 350 million years ago, the Cambrian, a long period of deposition in which hard sedimentary rocks were laid down, beginning about 400 million years ago and, the oldest of all, the pre-Cambrian, which is believed to have started at least 400 million years earlier still. From Newgale to Fishguard Bay there is a most complex rock structure of Ordovician dark and black shales and volcanic rocks, Cambrian slates, flags and sandstones, red, purple and grey grits, and pre-Cambrian tuffs. The capes from St. David's Head to Strumble Head are of igneous rock, mostly dolerite. The precipitous cliffs come to a climax in the massive Strumble Head. Boulder clay comes down to the sea in the few sections of low-lying coast. It is very noticeable in the lovely Whitesand Bay and at Porth

Melgan. From all these igneous and sedimentary rocks and from the boulder clay come pebbles of the most varied kind travelling northwards up the coast, held up for a long time by Strumble Head, but eventually rounding it and making their way up the gentler and less indented shores of Cardigan Bay. The beaches of Fishguard Bay and Newport Bay contain shingle derived from the diversified rocks of the Pembrokeshire coast.

We have now reached the southern end of Cardigan Bay. Its very long coast has many beautiful beaches, but it lacks the rugged grandeur of Pembrokeshire and it is much more uniform in its geological formation. All the way to Newquay the coast rocks consist of shales and sandstones. It is also a heavily-laden area of boulder clay, the outcome, it is believed, of the melting of the great ice-sheets that crossed the Irish Sea into Wales during the Ice Age. On many parts of the coast between Strumble Head and Cardigan it lies on the cliffs, sometimes coming down to the beaches. We shall find innumerable flints in the Cardigan Bay shingle. Nearly all of them have been washed out of the boulder clay, which was glacier-borne from the chalk of Ulster across the Irish Sea. Possibly chalk rocks now lying beneath that sea were also scoured by the glaciers.

This is a good pebble coast. Deep and narrow valleys (cwms) have cut down through the soft rocks to little bays. There is shingle in most of these. Some of the pebbles have come down by river from the plateau behind the coast. Some have come from the boulder clay and others have travelled up the coast from Pembrokeshire. Shingle bars have formed on the beaches of Cwm Tydi and Afon Soden.

The boulder clay grows thicker as we go northward. It forms the cliffs of New Quay Bay. There the shore has deposits of large pebbles from the heavy glacial deposit, with storm ridges of the larger stones at the back of the beaches. South of the harbour of the pleasant little town of Aberayron there is an ample spread of shingle, most of it boulder-clay pebbles. The glacial deposit goes on to a great depth, and with little interruption, from Aberayron to Llanrhystyd. The shingle is not continuous, but what there is is well worth inspection. Where the boulder clay does not overrun and obscure the cliffs steep rocks of grit emerge.

We are now nearing Aberystwyth, on the estuary of the rivers Rheidol and Ystwyth. A great accumulation of shingle has bent the mouth of the latter northward. There is smaller, but very good, shingle on the beaches to the north of the harbour. Apart from the numerous flints from the boulder clay and grit pebbles from the local rock there is a diversity of shingle from the igneous rocks of Pembrokeshire. Some nineteenth-century collectors reported that they had secured some small specimens of aquamarine at Aberystwyth. Aquamarine is the blue variety of beryl. It is not entirely impossible for pieces of this stone to have been found here, because it exists in the granite of the Mourne Mountains in N.E. Ireland and could have been transported by ice across the Irish Sea, but we think that even a prolonged search would bring little reward to-day.

High cliffs of grit run on to Borth. On the way we come to the very pleasant beach of Clarach Bay which has a substantial ridge of interesting shingle. There is plentiful shingle a little farther north, where Morfa Borth (or Borth Sands) extends for 2 miles until it joins the estuary of the river Dyfi to the south of Aberdovey. Across the estuary and spreading out at its mouth is a huge storm beach of large pebbles. Its growth is northward.

The coast rocks from Aberdovey northwards are of grit, slate and sandstone, changing to blue, blue-grey and black slates of the Cambrian Age before we reach Llwyngwril. Here is the beginning of a long shingle beach that eventually develops into the Ro Wen shingle spit that extends right up into the Mawddach estuary. It is a storm beach of large pebbles that have accumulated by northward longshore drifting. Sand-dunes cover parts of it and salt-marshes lie behind it. On the north side of the estuary a shingle ridge of boulder clay pebbles intermingled with shells runs out westward.

Barmouth lies just beyond it. The shingle of the beach off the promenade tends, unaccountably, to drift slightly to the south, that is, in the precisely opposite direction to the movement of beach material on all the rest of this coast.

Soon after we have gone beyond Barmouth we come to the beginning of Morfa Dyffryn, a great expanse of sand-dunes, blown sand and marsh extending for 6 miles from Llanaber to Llanbedr. Belts of shingle border it on the seaward side for parts of the way. The first belt begins near Llanaber railway station and runs for over a mile. Near Tyddyn Mawr it has suffered a broad breach, but it continues beyond the breach for more than a mile to the estuary of the little river Scethin. It has deflected the mouth of that river to the north, thus clearly demonstrating the northward drifting of beach material on this coast. The ridge resumes its northward journey on the other side of the Scethin and goes on for at least another mile. There is no more shingle of any appreciable extent until we come near to Mochras Island, locally known as Shell Island on account of the amazing number and variety of shells on its shores. The island is the remnant of a glacial moraine and is therefore a mass of boulder clay, a store-house of pebbles and boulders, which form a long spit running to the north-east to the estuary of the river Artro and resuming its way on the other side of the river right up to the boulder clay cliffs of Harlech.

Here we enter another region of sand-dunes, blown sand, salt-marshes and swamp, the great expanse of Morfa Harlech. In many ways it is like Morfa Dyffryn. Each is triangular in shape, with the apex of the triangle at the south, and each is a flat sandy foreland that has grown outwards from the former coast-line. But, whereas Morfa Dyffryn has large accumulations of shingle, Morfa Harlech possesses only one belt of ½-mile or so which fringes the sand-dunes at the southern end of the triangle. The pebbles are large and travel gradually northwards. As there is no break between them and the shingle spit that goes north rom Mochras Island, it would be true to say that the shingle of Morfa Dyffryn and that of Morfa Harlech are continuous.

We shall find no more pebbles until we reach the southern coast of the Lleyn Peninsula, which points like a finger, 30 miles long, down the Irish Sea. The drift of the pebbles on this coast is, of course, eastward, yet the supply is scanty at the eastern end, the corner at which the southern coast of Caernarvonshire meets the coast of Merionethshire. There is very little shingle in the coves of Borth-y-Gest and next to none borders the hard, firm sands of Morfa Bychan, but beyond Graig Ddu (Black Rock), which is a small headland of dolerite, there is a substantial increase. The source of the pebbles is the boulder clay beneath Criccieth promenade and in the cliffs east of the town. A bank of shingle runs thence up to Graig Ddu. It has dammed up a former bay and turned it into a fresh-water lake, Llyn Ystumllyn.

Criccieth Castle stands on hard rock, called rhyolite (from a Greek word meaning 'to flow'), of volcanic origin, containing the minerals, quartz and felspar. It was poured out on the surface in the form of lava.

The soft boulder clay then goes on westward to the headland of Pen-ychan. It provides numberless pebbles to form a belt of shingle from the promontory almost all the way to Criccieth. This shingle has pushed the mouth of the river Dwyfor eastward for a mile. The pebbles beyond Pen-ychan have been piled up by waves into high storm beaches. They remain in good supply for most of the way to Abererch, but diminish as we come nearer to Pwllheli. Behind the very pleasant beaches that lie to the west of that town is a layer of boulder clay, sand and gravel, but the headlands that separate the beaches are of hard, old rocks. Thus, Careg-yr-Imbill (Gimlet Rock), which protrudes between the two Pwllheli beaches, is a mass of dolerite, Careg-y-Defaid, the next headland to the west, consists of trachyte, a volcanic rock in which the principal mineral is a glassy kind of felspar, Llanbedrog Mountain at the southern end of Llanbedrog Beach is a headland of porphyritic granite, and the two promontories of St. Tudwal's Peninsula, Wylfa Head and Penkilan Head, consist of hard sandstone and flags. The three beaches of Llanbedrog,

Abersoch and Porth Caered are very attractive. Porth Caered contains the best shingle. The pebbles on all the beaches between Criccieth and St. Tudwal's Peninsula are of interesting variety, having come from the generous supplies of boulder clay and the hard rocks of the headlands.

We turn to the north-west after rounding Penkilan Head and enter Hell's Mouth or Porth Neigwl, a broad and pleasant bay that is not even remotely suggestive of eternal torment. Boulder-clay deposits of great thickness and a stretch of blown sand lie at the back of the beach. The softness of the bay is followed immediately by the hardness of the dolerite promontory to the west of it.

We are now near to Aberdaron Bay and the headland of Braich-y-Pwll, the 'Land's End' of North Wales. Here begins a stretch of the most ancient rocks, extending for more than 12 miles with little interruption along the northern coast of the Lleyn Peninsula. The predominant rock in this section is pre-Cambrian schist, highly laminated, flaky, greyish-green in colour and beautifully lustrous when freshly broken. Dykes of dolerite have intruded here and there. There is little shingle along this aged and very rocky coast, but some very good pebbles lie on the two beaches of Nevin which are just beyond the pre-Cambrian rocks. Of the two beaches, Porth Dinlleyn and Porth Nevin, the former is the bigger and has more shingle. Cliffs of boulder clay rise at the back of each. The pebbles from these and from the ancient rocks to the south-west make up a goodly assortment. The longshore drifting along this coast is from south-west to north-east. Very little beach material from the south Caernarvonshire and Cardigan Bay coasts travels around Braich-y-Pwll, because the Lleyn Peninsula is such a formidable barrier. The headland to the west of Porth Dinlleyn, Careg Ddu (Black Rock), also impedes, but far less effectively, the movement of beach material up the coast. Careg Ddu consists of volcanic rock, mostly pillow-lava, which we last saw at Pentire Point in Cornwall. Steep cliffs with very little beach beneath them are the main feature of the coast beyond Nevin to the Trevor granite quarries. These are cut in the most seaward of the three high peaks of Yr Eifl ('The Rivals' is an English mutilation of the Welsh name, but it is aptly descriptive of these peaks). Trevor granite is a beautiful stone and polishes well. Pebbles derived from it travel north-eastward up the Caernarvonshire coast.

The coast, up to Dinas Dinlle, near the south-western entrance to the Menai Straits, is almost wholly of boulder clay. It supplies pebbles in profusion to the belt of shingle that begins near Aber Desach and grows broader all the way to Dinas Dinlle. There it is piled up into a high storm beach. This ridge is the biggest on the northern coast of Caernarvonshire. Its pebbles, most of them extracted from the boulder clay, are also representative of the igneous, metamorphic and sedimentary rocks of the Lleyn Peninsula.

Leaving unexplored the rather muddy shores of the Menai Straits, we cross over to the south coast of Anglesey. This almost flat country appears featureless at first glance, but its coast is of charming variety and its rock structure is of bewildering complexity. The latter, indeed, is known to geologists as the Mona Complex (Mona being the Roman name of Anglesey). Much of its rock is pre-Cambrian and it has been so folded, crushed and sheared as to make the task of discovering the original stratification supremely difficult. The coastal rock pattern is too intricate to be unfolded here in any detail. We shall consider only the main features.

Longshore drifting from the Menai Straits up to Holy Island follows the north-western direction of the coast. Newborough Warren is a broad expanse of sand-dunes bordered with a little shingle, to which the pillow-lava, jasper and green schist of Llanddwyn Island make an agreeably coloured contribution. This side of Anglesey, especially Malldraeth Bay and Aberffraw Bay, is extremely sandy. We find little shingle until we reach Rhosneigr and Cymmyran Bay, where the sandy coast, especially of the bay, has a long belt of pebbles. They come from the boulder clay and from the rocks of mica schist, granite, sandstone, dolerite, gabbro and serpentine. The two last outcrop near the shores of the Strait that separates Holy Island from Anglesey. The serpentine is of the green variety, with a glossy surface and silky to the touch, but the weathered pebbles are dull. After the removal of the 'skin' and a little polishing, they display their true and lovely colouring.

The two best beaches on Holy Island itself are Borth Wen (Rhoscolyn) and Trearddur Bay, though neither possesses extensive shingle. The pebbles mostly come from the three main rocks that compose the island: mica schist, Holyhead quartzite and very hard, grey grit, all of them pre-Cambrian. The rocks of Newry Beach, Holyhead, are all of mica schist, but the beach is covered with fragments of the local quartzite, dumped there during the building of the breakwater in the middle of the last century. These fragments have not even yet been smoothed and rounded into true pebbles.

On the west coast of Anglesey the best bed of shingle is in the Porth Swtan end of Church Bay, where there are high cliffs of boulder clay from which the beach receives a large and varied quota. Rocks of pale yellow volcanic tuff, lying beneath the boulder clay, and adjacent strata of hard, dark grit (Skerries grit) and green schist also contribute their share. A few pebbles of jasper can usually be spotted by the patient collector.

The north coast has comparatively little shingle, but there is one good ridge $\frac{1}{2}$-mile long, banked up high above the arc of Cemlyn Bay. This is a storm beach inasmuch as it is the product of exceptional violence: that of 26th October 1859, which wrecked the *Royal Charter* at Moelfre with the loss of 455 lives. The ridge has produced the effect of a natural dam, for a lagoon now lies behind it, falling and rising with the tides. The top of the shingle ridge is about 20 feet above the high-water mark of the lagoon. Cemaes Bay shingle yields purple jasper.

Red Wharf Bay on the north-east coast is a very large expanse of slightly reddish sand. Its shingle is mostly drawn from the limestone cliffs to the west of it and from the eastward drifting pebbles formed from the granite, green schist and mica schist of the north-east Anglesey coast. There is also a fairly plentiful supply of chert from the limestone.

Coming back to Carnarvonshire again across the north-eastern entrance to the Menai Straits, we must go on to the beaches of Llanfairfechan and Penmaenmawr to find any shingle deserving of comment. Rocks of the Ordovician Age, shales, grits and slates lie behind the beaches, but Penmaenmawr Mountain is a huge mass of igneous rock, diorite, which is used largely for road metal and railway-track ballast. It is a very hard and close-grained stone of greyish-blue. Some large amount has made its way to the beach during the loading of ships at the quarry quays and has been rolled and rounded into pebbles. The shingle of the Penmaenmawr beach lines the coast up to the flat plain of Conway Morfa, the sand and alluvium of the Conway estuary, now largely grass-covered. Beyond the estuary is the Creuddyn Peninsula, a foreland terminating in two bold headlands, the Great Orme and the Little Orme, with the seaside resort of Llandudno lying between them. Both of these headlands consist of limestone. The Great Orme, thrusting itself far out to sea, acts as a great groyne against the eastward drifting of the Anglesey and North Carnarvonshire pebbles. Llandudno has two beaches: the West shore facing Anglesey and the beach between the two Ormes facing north. The former is of sand, which at low water seems to stretch out far to the south-west. It must have been here that

The Walrus and the Carpenter were walking close at hand
and

wept like anything to see such quantities of sand

for Lewis Carroll stayed at the Gogarth Abbey Hotel on this shore and roamed about it with little Alice Liddell, the original 'Alice'.

The shingle of the other beach has many pebbles of Great Orme limestone, with some of grit, shale, slate, diorite, etc., that have contrived to make their way round from the other side of Conway Morfa.

Limestone pebbles from the Little Orme feed the beaches of Rhos-on-Sea and Colwyn Bay. The long promenade now protects the cliffs of boulder clay between those two places. Before it was built, there was considerable erosion and a wealth of pebbles was washed out from the clay. The promenade now reaches to Old Colwyn, so the Colwyn Bay shingle is not as plentiful as it once was. However, it is still fairly extensive and is varied enough to be interesting. Limestone, of course, is the main contributory, but there are still many boulder-clay pebbles left, including some good specimens of quartz. At the east end of the bay is another limestone headland, Penmaen Head, from which pebbles of that rock travel eastward to add to the beach material of Llandulas and Abergele. Boulder clay to a great depth lies between these beaches and the hills inland, so there is no shortage of shingle. Together with the sand from the dunes on the shore between Abergele and Rhyl it has deflected, by eastward drifting, the mouth of the river Clywd one mile to the east. Groynes at Prestatyn check the drifting to some extent and help to deepen the beach there. The drifting comes to an end in the high storm ridges off the Point of Air.

And here we almost come to the end of our quest for pebbles on the west coast. The Point of Air marks the eastern end of the great estuary of the river Dee. On the Welsh side there are mudflats, marshes and alluvium all the way. The shores of the Wirral Peninsula on the other side are more refreshing. A boulder-clay cliff runs behind them as far as West Kirby and provides shingle between Neston and West Kirby. The great dunes of Hoylake and Wallasey are the main feature of the north coast of the peninsula, but we have far to go before we come upon any extensive beds of shingle. Quickly passing the Mersey estuary and the completely industrialized coast of the Liverpool area, whence runs a long coast of sand-dunes to Southport, we come to the peat of the Ribble estuary. There is some shingle on its northern shore. It has drifted from the beaches on the south of Blackpool along the shore of St. Anne's towards the salt-marshes of Lytham and beyond. In doing this the pebbles from the coast immediately south of Blackpool have, for a reason yet to be discovered, broken the general rule of longshore drifting on the west coast. The shingle comes to an end at South Shore. The Blackpool beach between South and North Shore is wholly of sand. Then the shingle begins again and increases in extent as we get near to Cleveleys. The supply from there to Fleetwood is bountiful. Most of the pebbles come from the boulder-clay cliffs that form the Lancashire coastline north of Blackpool. They contain some pebbles brought down by glaciers from the Cumberland and Westmorland mountains, so much of the shingle is of grit, limestone, sandstone and granite and other igneous rocks.

The coast makes a turn to the right before we reach Fleetwood, which stands at the entrance to the Wyre estuary. The river runs out between mud-banks and salt-marshes. So far all the coast of Lancashire has been bounded by soft material: boulder clay, dunes and marsh, except, of course, where man has built sea-walls and promenades. The first outcrop of solid rock that we come to all the way from the Mersey is some red sandstone at Cockersand Abbey, south of the Lune estuary, and here there is a good shingle beach. We are now within sight of Morecambe Bay. In one respect this large bay resembles the Wash: on some of its long coast the distance between high- and low-water marks is several miles. There are great expanses of sand and silt and there is a large spread and depth of boulder clay. To find shingle beds we must pass across the bay to Walney Island.

This 8-mile-long and narrow island that provides a natural breakwater for the protection of Barrow-in-Furness must have come into existence when the glaciers on this part of the coast melted, for it consists of boulder clay, sand and gravel. There is glacial shingle on its beaches and ridges of that shingle extend from its northern and southern ends. Of the four islands to the east of Walney, Sheep, Roa and Foulney are all composed of shingle, and Piel is almost all shingle. The exception to the general rule about longshore drifting on the west coast begins to apply at Walney Island. From St. Bees Head to the island the drifting is southward.

Great spreads of sand, the Duddon Sands, lie north of Walney Island at the broad mouth of the river Duddon. The seemingly endless boulder clay goes on and on, but it has one interruption at Holbarrow Point at the entrance to the estuary. It is an outcrop of limestone. The pebbles from the boulder clay have planed down the rock to a smooth platform here by their rolling. When we have crossed the estuary our course lies along a smooth, flat coast, only slightly indented. It is lined with cliffs of boulder clay. Sand and sand-dunes increase as we approach Eskmeals. There is a narrow estuary to the north of Eskmeals through which the three rivers, Esk, Mite and Irt, all come out to sea. The outflow of the Irt is turned 2 miles to the south-east by a long and wide spit of sand and shingle, called Drigg Point. Nearly all the pebbles have come from the boulder clay. For the next 4 miles, to Seascale, there is nothing but sand and dunes lining a dead straight coast, but a mile or so beyond Seascale we come to another joint river mouth, that of the Calder and the Ehen. A spit of shingle surmounted by sand-dunes keeps the Ehen inshore for a distance of 2 miles until it is forced to join the Calder.

The straight coast of low cliffs of boulder clay continues to St. Bees Head. At long last we see high cliffs of solid rock. There are two points to remember about St. Bees Head. It is the first promontory of high solid rock north of Penmaen Head at Colwyn Bay; and it marks the point at which the northward drifting of beach material up the west coast starts again. The fine cliffs of St. Bees Head are of hard red sandstone. Other good cliffs of hard limestone follow on as far as Saltom Bay. The cliff line is lowered to beach level only in Fleswick Bay. Here is a pebble beach on which the collector should linger, for among its pebbles of limestone, sandstone and shale from the local rocks are many from the boulder clay, brought down by the glaciers of Cumberland and south-west Scotland. These include numerous pebbles of igneous rock and quartz in several of its chalcedonic varieties. Some good specimens of agate, jasper and carnelian can be found. This beach deserves all the attention we can give to it, because it is also the last shingle deposit of interest to the collector on this coast. The shore from Whitehaven Harbour to Maryport is blackened by slag heaps, mine-refuse dumps, drifting coal-dust and pebbles of blast-furnace slag. Owing to the northward drift this rubbish travels as far as the Solway shore.

The last miles of our tour are along a low, flat coast of boulder clay fringed here and there by dunes, sand-hills, marshes, alluvium and peat-bogs. There are a few ridges of shingle and boulders, but the only interesting features are the sections of raised beach. These are prominent to the north of Workington, Allonby and Beckfoot. Indeed, raised beach deposits are visible almost all the way from Workington to Beckfoot, running parallel with the present-day beach and touching it at those points where there are high storm beaches. We find the raised beach again near Beckfoot, whence it goes on through Silloth to Grune Point on the far side of Skinburness Marsh. As we enter the narrow and inner part of the Solway Firth we find it between Anthorn and Bowness. For most of their course the raised beaches are elevated about 14–15 feet above the modern beaches, but at Grune Point the shingle of the raised beach is actually growing with some rapidity as the result of longshore drifting.

VI

PEBBLE-HUNTING AS A HOBBY

How to classify your collection

O ne of the advantages of pebble-collecting as a hobby is that it is one of the most leisurely of part-time pursuits, making little demand upon one's patience and still less upon one's physical energy. If the collector lives far from the coast, he must, of course, conduct his beach peregrinations within the limits of his annual seaside holiday, having made sure that the resort of his choice possesses a good shingle beach or is within very easy reach of one. If, however, he is fortunate enough to live on the coast and near to such a beach, he can make his forays when time, weather and mood are all entirely to his liking. A fine and not too windy day in winter, when he has the whole shore to himself, provides the happiest conditions for the assiduous collector. Unless he is one of those rare unfortunates who suffer from the fear of open spaces, he will agree with Byron that:

> *There is a rapture on the lonely shore,*
> *There is society where none intrudes,*
> *By the deep sea, and music in its roar.*

The pastime commends itself on other grounds. For example, it is very inexpensive. There is no market in pebbles. They are there for the taking. Given sufficient practice, discernment and discrimination, the collector can acquire an array of choice specimens at no cost whatsoever. Naturally, he will have to pay

144

if he wishes to have some of his collection professionally cut and polished, but he can have this done for a very modest sum. Then, again, the cult does not demand membership of any society, whose annual subscription he must pay or whose quarterly journal he feels duty-bound to read. There is no scanning of advertisement columns for bargains nor are there any pilgrimages to sale rooms.

Once he has begun to pursue the hobby he will almost certainly feel an urge to add to his knowledge of geology, and will not be content with the mere rudiments which have been set out in the third chapter of this book. In doing so, he will experience an ever-quickening and refreshing interest, not only in his pebble expeditions, but in all his walks abroad, for he will be able to read the 'sermons in stones, books in the running brooks', as the enthralling record of the creation of the rocks gradually unfolds itself to him.

Many geologists and mineralogists make their own collections of rock specimens, but they restrict their choice to fragments of rock that have been freshly fractured and, in consequence, have an unweathered surface. They also try to ensure that the piece they select is representative of the whole mass of rock from which they hammered it out, or, if the mass has variations, that they secure enough specimens to represent those variations.

The pebble-collector cannot adopt that procedure, as all his pebbles have acquired to some extent a disguise in the form of a 'skin' as the result of the rolling and weathering they have endured. They must appear in his collection as he found them. They will, of course, look all the better for a wash and brush-up, but this will not rid them of their disguise. However, he can, and should, emulate the example of the conscientious geologist in one respect: he should strive to gather two pebbles of each kind in his collection, retaining one in its beach disguise and breaking the other in order to display a fresh, unweathered surface. The two should lie side by side in his cabinet. From the broken surface of one he can learn much about the composition, texture and colouring of the rock from which it came; from the unbroken and disguised surface of the other he will be able to memorize the appearance of a beach pebble of that rock.

If the broken pebble's texture, colour or fossilized contents are especially pleasing to him, he can, of course, acquire a third pebble of that kind and have it cut and polished.

In compiling and arranging his collection he must try to work to a plan from the outset. Here are a few suggestions:

Firstly, he can decide to make a large and comprehensive collection, fully representative of all but the very rare rocks. Only the more determined, energetic and conscientious collectors would set themselves this task, but it is an admirable objective. If he attempts it he should follow faithfully the orthodox classification of rocks, allotting separate compartments to igneous, metamorphic and sedimentary rocks, and also keeping separate the various divisions of the three main classes, e.g. the division of the igneous class into volcanic (extrusive) rocks and plutonic (intrusive) rocks. He must also display specimens of every common variety of even one kind of rock, e.g. limestone (oolitic, dolomitic or magnesian, coral, crinoidal limestone, etc.).

Secondly, if he has neither the leisure nor the desire to be so thorough, he can adopt the sound plan of making his collection as representative as possible of one good beach or of several good beaches. But here, again, he must try to classify his specimens in accordance with approved geological principles.

Thirdly, if his interest should lie wholly or mainly in one group of rocks, he may limit his collection to pebbles of those rocks and still be able to display a good assortment. Some collectors, for instance, find delight only in siliceous rocks, possibly because the members of the silica family present a glittering array, or perhaps because some of them can claim to be called semi-precious stones. Classification, in this case, is simple, as only one main mineral is involved. The sub-divisions are merely the names of the pebbles, e.g. quartz, chalcedony, agate, carnelian, jasper, etc.

Other collectors are unmoved by any rocks other than the

fossiliferous kind, as their interests are more biological than geological, or, in other words, they prefer the organic to the inorganic. It is preferable to classify a collection of this kind under the headings of the fossils themselves rather than of the rocks that contain them, as the fossils are many but the kinds of fossil-bearing rock are comparatively few, e.g. limestone, chalk, flint, chert, shale, sandstone, grit, marl and clay.

Accompanying every pebble must be a little card on which the collector has entered the name of the rock, the beach and the date of the find. If the beach is a long ridge or belt of shingle, some rough indication of the position occupied by the pebble on it should be given. The memory can be very untrustworthy if bags of pebbles are left unlabelled for even a day or two after a visit to several beaches, so, to ensure correct identification, the collector who intends to visit several beaches in the course of a day or holiday must take with him several stout paper bags and mark on each of them that he fills the name of the beach and the date. If he visits one beach only, he should mark the bag at once. Should he fail to do so and the bag is left lying about, pending a spare hour when he can add the contents to the cabinet, he will not be completely certain of the beach whence they came.

The word 'cabinet' has been freely used in this book, but this does not imply that ownership of a geological display cabinet is essential. Naturally, it is very desirable, but, failing it, there are other articles that will serve the purpose moderately well. Some of them can be bought at furniture sale rooms or second-hand shops, others can be made at home by collectors with an aptitude for joinery. Old filing cabinets are not to be despised; glass-fronted cupboards, fitted with a good number of shelves, all of little depth, are excellent. A box or chest in which wooden trays lie, one above the other, each tray being divided by thin partitions into 32 or 40 compartments, will provide room for a fairly big collection; but, for the collector who likes to have his specimens on permanent view, there is nothing to equal the glass-topped, shallow showcase.

APPENDIX

A Book list for those who wish to make further and deeper studies of geology in general or of sea-beaches in particular

1. SEA-BEACHES

The Coastline of England and Wales, by J. A. Steers (Cambridge University Press, 1946).

This is the authoritative and the only comprehensive work on the subject. Professor Steers, who is President of St. Catharine's College, Cambridge, has surveyed the whole coastline in detail. His great book is the outcome of this scientific survey and of many years' study of coastal evolution. In it he has much to say about the growth and movement of shingle spits and ridges, but shingle is only one of the many coastal features which he describes and explains in lucid detail. There are fascinating chapters on recent vertical movements of the shoreline, the evolution and erosion of sand-dunes, the development of creeks, the growth of marshes and the vegetation of dunes and marshes.

The author has relied upon Professor Steers's survey in the writing of Chapter V, especially in respect of those parts of the coast which he (the author) has yet to visit.

The Sea Coast, by J. A. Steers (The New Naturalist Series, Collins, 1953).

A much smaller book, intended for the more general reader, The chapters on sand and shingle spits, salt marshes and major shingle structures must on no account be missed. Both this and the larger work are finely and generously illustrated. The many maps and diagrams clearly elucidate the text.

The Physical Basis of Geography: An Outline of Geomorphology, by Dr. S. W. Wooldridge and R. S. Morgan (Longmans. Green & Co., 1937).

This is the standard work on geomorphology. Though it is prescribed for students preparing for an honours degree in geography, it has a strong appeal to the serious reader who has no examination in view. Only one chapter relates to sea-beaches (XXI—Marine Erosion and Shore Lines), but the remainder of the book cannot fail to hold the attention of all readers who wish to become more familiar with that borderland in which geography and geology meet.

2. GEOLOGY

Britain's Structure and Scenery, by Dr. L. Dudley Stamp (The New Naturalist Series, Collins, 1946).

The best of all introductions to the geology and the resultant scenery of this country. It tells in simple language the story of the structure of Britain through all the geological ages. The coloured plates and other illustrations are of the highest merit and the maps and diagrams of the utmost assistance to the reader. Those who prefer to begin their study of geology with a more elementary book should first read:

Physical Geology and Geography, by the same author (Longmans, 1938).

Geology for Beginners, by W. W. Watts (Macmillan & Co., 1942), is a very sound introductory textbook.

The Living Landscape of Britain, by Walter Shepherd (Faber and Faber, 1952).

A Textbook of Geology, by P. Lake and R. H. Rastall (Fifth Edition: Edward Arnold, 1941).

This is one of the standard textbooks. It is definitely not a bedside book, as it is written for the serious student, and it is highly recommended to all who wish to progress far beyond the rudiments.

Geology and Scenery in England and Wales, by Dr. A. E. Trueman (A Pelican Book, 1949).

Avoiding technical terms as far as possible, this is an attractive account of how the principal features of English and Welsh scenery came into existence. It describes these features very clearly, district by district, and relates them in simple phraseology to the geological causes that gave rise to them.

Geology in the Service of Man, by W. G. Fearnsides and Dr. O. M. B. Balman (A Pelican Book, 1945), is another book for the layman.

After a very readable introduction to the principles of geology it deals with some of the important applications of the science. It contains a masterly summary of geological history and an excellent chapter on the construction and use of geological maps.

The Earth and its Mysteries, by Dr. G. W. Tyrell (G. Bell & Sons, Ltd., 1953).

An excellent introduction to geology and geomorphology, fully and clearly illustrated. This is the most recent work on the subject and its account of the results of the latest geological research e.g. the methods of determining the age of the earth, is therefore of especial interest and value.

An introduction to Palaeontology, by A. M. Davies (T. Murby and Co., 1920).

An essential book for those collectors whose main interest is in fossils and a most desirable one for all, as a knowledge of the fossils that appear in the rocks of the several geological ages helps the student to fix the comparative age of the rocks and to identify them more easily.

OFFICIAL PUBLICATIONS AND MAPS

The authorities of the Geological Survey have divided Great Britain into eighteen regions, for every one of which they have provided a descriptive and explanatory 'Regional Handbook' at a very modest price. All who aspire to become familiar with the geology of their own part of the country and with the coastal rocks of the sea-beaches on which they search for pebbles are most strongly urged to secure the relative Handbooks. The language is much simpler than that of the more advanced textbooks, but it contains enough technical terminology to baffle the reader who has not already grasped the rudiments of geology. A study of one of the introductory books recommended above should therefore come first. The Handbooks are obtainable from H.M. Stationery Office, Kingsway, London, W.C.2, or through any bookseller.

The Geological Survey of Great Britain issues a geological counterpart of every one-inch-to-the-mile Ordnance Survey Map, so covering the whole country. The one-inch scale is large enough to provide sufficient geological detail for all general purposes. There are two series of these excellent maps—the Old and the New. All the unsold copies of the Old series, together with the plates from which they were printed, were destroyed in the Southampton blitz, when the headquarters of the Ordnance Survey was hit. Consequently, only second-hand copies of the Old series are now obtainable. The New series, colour-printed, is now appearing as, one by one, the areas are being re-surveyed, but some years must pass before the series is complete.

The Survey also publishes geological maps of smaller scale and therefore covering a much larger area. The $\frac{1}{4}$-inch-to-the-mile map is very useful, though, of course, it omits much of the detail that the one-inch map can show. For the student who requires a map of the whole country the Survey's 'Ten-Mile' map is most serviceable. Two sheets cover all Scotland, England and Wales, the border between the two running east–west from Eskmeals in Cumberland to Cloughton (north of Scarborough).

All these maps are beautifully coloured and most accurately annotated. They are obtainable from Edward Stanford, Ltd., 12 Long Acre, London, W.C.2, or through any bookseller.

INDEX

Moles, 46
Mona Complex, 137
Moraines, 124, 134
Morecambe Bay, 141
Morfa Borth, 133
Morfa Bychan, 135
Morfa Dyffryn, 134
Morfa Harlech, 134
Morgan, R. S., 149
Morte Bay, 127
Morte Point, 127
Mount's Bay, 123
Mourne Mountains, 50, 133
Mousehole, 124
Mull, Island of, 81
Mullion, 123
Mumbles Head, 129
Mupe Bay, 119
Musselwick Bay, 131

National Trust, 108
Natural History Museum, 66
Navax Point, 125
Naze, The, 112
Needles, The, 116–17
Ness, The, 121
Nevin, 136, 137
Newgale, 131
Newborough Warren, 137
Newhaven, 114
Newlyn, 124
Newquay (Cardiganshire), 132
Newquay (Cornwall), 125
Newry Beach, 138
Norfolk, 44, 106–10
North Foreland, 107, 112
Niton, 117
North Sea, 17, 41, 42, 45, 95, 106, 107, 109
Northumberland, 100–3, 104
North Weir Point, 25
Norway, 17
Norwich Red Crag, 109

Oberstein, 87
Obsidian, 79, 94
Oddicombe, 121
Old Colwyn, 140
Old Harry Rocks, 118
Olivine, 67
Onyx, 85, 88

Oolite, 53
Ordnance Survey, 151
Ordovician Age, 131, 139
Orford Ness, 25, 110
Orme, Great, 139
Orme, Little, 139, 140
Orwell, River, 111
Otter, River, 24
Oxwich Bay, 129
Oystermouth, 129

Padstow Bay, 126
Pagham Harbour, 116
Paignton, 121
Palaeontology, 70
Par, 123
Park Head, 125
Parret, River, 127, 128
Peebles, cylindrical, 21, 65, 66; flattened ovoid, 21, 22, 65, 66; Lake, 29–30; ovoid, 21, 22, 66, 67, 127; piriform, 67; porphyritic, 69, 75, 124; river, 30; spherical, 21, 22, 66
Pegwell Bay, 111
Pembrokeshire, 128, 129–32, 133
Penarth Head, 128
Pendeen Watch, 125
Pendine, 129
Penkilan Head, 135, 136
Penmaen Head, 140, 142
Penmaenmawr, 139
Pennines, 54
Pentire Point, 125, 126, 136
Pen-ychan, 135
Peppercombe, 126
Penzance, 124
Perran Beach, 125
Persia, 96
Petrological microscope, 61
Pevensey, 25, 114
Pevensey Levels, 114
Piel Island, 141
Plymouth, 122
Plymouth Sound, 123
Pomerania, 95
Poole Harbour, 118
Porlock Bay, 127
Port Eynon, 129
Porthcawl, 128
Porth Caered, 136

INDEX